THE TALE OF
THE ELOQUENT PEASANT

THE TALE OF
THE ELOQUENT PEASANT

Edited by

R. B. Parkinson

GRIFFITH INSTITUTE

OXFORD

British Library Cataloguing in Publication Data
Parkinson, Richard Bruce, 1963–
    The tale of the eloquent peasant.
    I. Title
    398.210962

    ISBN 0 90041 661 0
        0 90041 660 2 paperback

Set in Lasercomp Bembo
at Oxford University Computing Service

Printed in Great Britain
at the Alden Press, Oxford

CONTENTS

LIST OF FIGURES

PREFACE

The present work originated as the introduction to a doctoral thesis in the Faculty of Oriental Studies at the University of Oxford (*The Tale of the Eloquent Peasant: A Commentary*, 1988). It is intended to fill the gap left by the unfinished state of A. M. Blackman's *Middle-Egyptian Stories*, of which the 'Story of the Eloquent Peasant' was to form pp. 48–83, by providing a parallel text and a description of the manuscripts. The new line numbering adopted here conforms with modern practice, and is necessary for indicating the structure of the manuscripts (see 1.3); concordances of old and new numbering systems are given in 1.8.

In preparing this work I have benefited from the advice of Mark Smith (Oxford), with whom I first read the text, and John Baines who became the supervisor of my thesis. I am especially grateful to him for all his assistance and support as well as for his meticulous editing and constant availability for discussion. My thanks are due to Ingeborg Müller (Staatliche Museen, Berlin) for providing invaluable photographs of the Berlin manuscripts and for assistance in collation, to S. Quirke (British Museum) for help with P Butler and the Ramesseum papyri, to William Voelkle (Pierpont Morgan Library) for information about the Amherst fragments, and to A. F. Shore (School of Archaeology and Oriental Studies, University of Liverpool) for allowing me to consult and cite Blackman's unpublished transcription. I am also grateful to the Griffith Institute, where most of this was written, for its assistance and for access to unpublished notes by Barns, Gunn, and Newberry, as well as to Yvonne Harpur (Oxford) for all her technical assistance in preparing the text and for her encouragement. In drawing the transcription, I have used a system developed by my father, to whose artistry I am indebted. I am especially grateful to him and to my mother for their constant support. Finally my thanks are due to Christian Klotz and Tim Reid for their friendship.

R. B. Parkinson
University College, Oxford

PREFACE TO SECOND PRINTING

For this reprint, an error in transcription has been corrected (B1 236, p. 32), some notes have been revised (p. 6a n. 2.a, 41a n. 5.a, 45a n. 2.a), and a major new reading by Jürgen Osing is included in the notes (B2 95, p. 46a).

A recent re-examination of the original has shown that the 'strip of papyrus' on P. Berlin 3023 mentioned on p. xiv is not a reinforcement strip placed over a kollesis (K⁵) as I had thought, but is the result of two separate rolls with ruled lines having been joined together to form P. Berlin 3022, with the re-used roll to the right of K⁵ being glued under a kollesis (right over left) of another re-used roll, producing three layers of papyrus at this point.

For further discussion of the provenance of the 'Berlin Library', see now R. B. Parkinson, 'The Missing Beginning of *The Dialogue of a Man and his Ba*: P. Amherst III and the History of the "Berlin Library"', *ZÄS* 130 (2003) 120–33; R. B. Parkinson and Patricia Usick, 'A Note on the "Berlin Library" and the British Museum', *GM* 197 (2003) 93–7. I consider the relationship between the B1 and B2 manuscripts in this library in 'The History of a Poem: Middle Kingdom Literary Manuscripts and Their Reception', in Günter Burkard et al. (eds.), *Kon-Texte: Akten des Symposiums "Spurensuche: Altägypten im Spiegel seiner Texte", München 2. bis 4. Mai 2003* (ÄAT 60, 2004) 51–63.

On p. xxxiii, the bibliography should include the following:

Berlev, Oleg Dmitrievich 1969, '"Sokol, plyvushchii v lad'e": ieroglif i bog', *Vestnik Drevnei Istorii* 1 (107) 3–30.

R.B.P.
October 2005

INTRODUCTION

1.1   THE MANUSCRIPTS

The *Tale of the Eloquent Peasant* is preserved in four fragmentary Middle Kingdom manuscripts, which are here described and transcribed:

B1	Papyrus Berlin 3023
B2	Papyrus Berlin 3025
A	Papyrus Amherst I = Fragments A–E of B1
	Papyrus Amherst II = Fragments F–G of B2
Bt	Papyrus Butler (recto) = Papyrus BM 10274
R	Papyrus Ramesseum A = Papyrus Berlin 10499

The Berlin papyri were first published in 1859 (*LD*), supplemented in 1892 by the publication of Papyrus Butler (Griffith 1892), and in 1899 by Newberry's publication of the Amherst fragments (Newberry 1899). Chabas was the first to study the text and to recognize its character, translating almost 90 lines in 1863 (1863:294–303; 1864). Twenty years later Maspero produced the first attempt at an extensive translation (up to B1 118, 1882:173–84), followed in 1895 by Petrie's free paraphrase (1895:61–80; incorporating Griffith's interpretations: 4) and, in 1899, by Erman's translation (Erman & Krebs 1899:46–53). By 1904 Vogelsang had begun his work which culminated in his *Kommentar zu den Klagen des Bauern* (1913), and in 1908 he collaborated with Gardiner on the official publication of the two Berlin and the Ramesseum manuscripts, with a continuous translation; this edition has been the basis for all subsequent studies.

While Vogelsang was preparing his valuable *editio princeps*, Lexa wrote a series of notes on the Tale (1912), which were not mentioned by Vogelsang, and their reliance on extensive emendation was felt to justify his omission (cf. G 1913:264; reviews of Vogelsang: Grapow 1913, Maspero 1914). All subsequent translations have relied heavily on Vogelsang's pioneering work. Gardiner followed Vogelsang with a series of notes, which he did not complete (1913–14, covering R 1.1–B1 205); his revised analysis of the Tale appeared as an annotated translation in *JEA* 9 (1923). This contained many improved readings and renderings and is the last major advance in interpretation. Ten years later, Suys published his *Étude sur le conte du fellah plaideur* (1933), based on new and largely erroneous readings of the manuscripts. He dwelt on points of divergence with previous work, but, in Blackman's words, he 'added little of value to the work of his two chief predecessors' (1934:218). In 1986 E. Perry produced another commentary as a doctoral dissertation (*A Critical Study of the Eloquent Peasant*), which does not include a transcription of the texts, and advances the understanding of the text on only a few points. As stated in the Preface, the Tale was the subject of my doctoral thesis (Oxford, 1988). Since 1933 there have been several important studies of individual passages and aspects, as well as annotated translations (most importantly Lichtheim 1973:169–84).

1.2 PROVENANCE AND SUBSEQUENT HISTORY

P Berlin 3023 (B1) and 3025 (B2)

B1 and B2 were bought for the Berlin Museum with other literary papyri at the sale of the Athanasi collection in June 1843 (Sotheby's, London: VG:6). The other papyri were P Berlin 3022 (*Sinuhe*) and 3024 (*Lebensmüder* and *The Tale of the Herdsman*); the provenance was not recorded. Their common literary character suggests that they were discovered together as a library (Goedicke 1970:1; Simpson 1972:70), probably in a tomb, as were the Ramesseum Papyri. This assumption is supported by the fact that B1 and P Berlin 3022 (*Sinuhe*) were written by the same scribe (Möller 1927a:15); both manuscripts show an idiosyncratic orthography of *srw* 'officials' (Text 15a.9.a). The other papyri, which Möller believed to be by a different scribe but of the same period, are so similar that Vogelsang and Gardiner (VG:6) considered that they might almost be from the same hand; this is particularly true of P Berlin 3024 (*Lebensmüder*) and 3022 (*Sinuhe*: Goedicke 1970:3 n.13). The Athanasi collection included pieces most probably from Thebes (Goedicke 1970:1 n.4; cf. Perry 1986:21), and Thebes was suggested as the find-site by Newberry, who described their discovery as being 'many years ago in some locality, perhaps Thebes, in Upper Egypt' (1899:9).

P Amherst

Papyri Amherst I and II are fragments of B1 and B2. Identified by Newberry in 1891 and transcribed by Griffith (1892:452, 461–4), they were fully published in collotype and transcription by Newberry in 1899 with fragments of P Berlin 3022 (*Sinuhe*) and of an unidentified text (a wisdom text: Helck 1982a:673; Posener 1951a:39 no.32). Newberry did not realize that A II was a part of B2. 'When and where Lord Amherst procured them is unfortunately not certain, but it seems probable that they were obtained with the collections of Mr. Lieder of Cairo in the year 1861' (Newberry 1899:9). Lieder worked in Cairo from 1825 to 1862, dying three years later (Dawson and Uphill 1969:179). The date of A's acquisition was given by Griffith in 1892 as 'about thirty years ago' (452). He noted another possible source for the fragments, the Hartwell Museum of Dr Lee (1783–1866), but in Bonomi's catalogue of that collection (1858) nothing identifiable with them is mentioned. If one assumes that they had been in Athanasi's possession with the Berlin papyri, rather than having been dispersed by the orginal finders, they were presumably acquired from Athanasi ultimately before 1843; Lieder could easily have dealt with him at this period, whereas one might expect Lee to have acquired them by 1858, which he apparently did not. Lieder is thus the most likely source. In 1912 they were purchased by the Pierpont Morgan Library, New York (a new catalogue of the collection is being prepared by Ogden Goelet).

This group of fragments demonstrates again the close asssociation of the Berlin Papyri at all stages of their history, supporting the library hypothesis.

P Butler

Bt was first brought to notice and partly published in 1864 by Goodwin, who noted that it was then labelled 'Butler 527' and hypothesized that it had been bought at the Athanasi sale of 1843, like B1 and B2 (1864:250). This suggestion was based on his assumption that it was written by the same scribe as B1 (1864:251), which is very unlikely. Bishop Samuel Butler (1774–1839) had acquired it at the sale of the third Salt collection in 1835. In the catalogue it is item 417, 'a papyrus in the Enchorial character, upright lines, 6 in. broad and about 2 ft. long...... *Thebes*. £5.7s.6d' (Athanasi 1836:183; identification confirmed by British Museum records). In 1840 the papyrus was sold to the British Museum. Thirty years after Goodwin, it was more fully published by Griffith with a copy by Newberry (Griffith 1892:pl. 1–4), later collated by Gunn (MS, date uncertain); a published photograph is James *et al.* 1979:100 fig. 39. There are plans to publish a full edition.

P Ramesseum A

R was found by Quibell in 1896 in a late Middle Kingdom tomb under the magazines of the Ramesseum (1898:3–4; pl. 1; *PM* I², 679; Kemp & Merrillees 1980:166). At the foot of the tomb-shaft, was a box ('18 × 12 × 12 ″') with a jackal drawn on the lid, presumably left there by robbers. Inside was a bundle of pen reeds and the following papyri, as numbered by Gardiner:

A	*The Eloquent Peasant* and *Sinuhe* (P Berlin 10499)
B	Dramatic Papyrus (P BM 10610, Berlin fragments; Sethe 1928b:pl. 1–22; G 1955a:8, 17–18 fig. 2)
C	Semna Despatches, with magical texts on the verso (P BM 10752; Smither 1945; G 1955a:8, 11, pl. 29–32; Spanel 1984)
D	Onomasticon (P Berlin 10495; G 1947:6–23, pl. 1–6; G 1955a:8)

E   Funerary liturgy, with a business text on the verso (P BM 10753; G 1955a:8, 11, pl. 28; G 1955b; Helck 1981)

I   *The Discourse of Sisobek* (P BM 10754; G 1955a:8, pl. 1–2; Barns 1956:1–10, pl. 1–6)

II   Wisdom text (P BM 10755; G 1955a:8–9, pl. 3–6; Barns 1956:11–14, pl. 7–9)
III   Medico-magical text (P BM 10756; G 1955a:9, 17, pl. 7–10, 63–4; Barns 1956:15–23, pl. 10–15, 24–5)
IV   Magico-medical text (P BM 10757; G 1955a:9, pl. 10–14; Barns 1956:24–9, pl. 163-20, 25)
V   Magical text (P BM 10758; G 1955a:9, pl. 15–17; Barns 1956:30–34, pl. 21–3)
VI   Hymns to Sobek (P BM 10759, 10760.2, 5, 7; G 1955a:10, pl. 18–21; G 1957b)
VII   Magical (recto) and mathematical (verso) texts (P BM 10760.1, 4, 6, 8–11; G 1955a:10–11, pl. 22–7)
VIII–XI Magical texts (P BM 10761–4; G 1955a:11–14, pl. 33–44)
XII   Invocations to demons (P BM 10765; G 1955a:14, pl. 45)
XIII   Magical text (recto) and a diary of an embalmment (? verso) (P BM 10766; G 1955a:14–15 fig. 1, pl. 46)
XIV–VI Magical texts (P BM 10767–9; G 1955a:14–16, pl. 46–61)
XVII   Protection against the epagomenal days (P BM 10770; G 1955a:16)
XVIII   Nubian despatches (P BM 10771; G 1955a:17, pl. 62)
        P BM 10772 comprises three frames of fragments of magical texts and a Nubian despatch

Scattered around the box were the following items, numbered after Quibell 1898:3, pl. 2–3:

1–3   Fragments of four ivory 'wands' (Manchester University Museum 1799, 1800, 1801; H. Altenmüller 1965:II, 108–11; Bosse-Griffiths 1977:102, fig. 1)
4   Bronze uraeus entangled in a mass of hair (Fitzwilliam Museum, Cambridge, E.63.1896; Bourriau 1988:113 [no. 100])
5   Faience lion (Manchester University Museum 1839)
6   Faience ape and beads
7   White faience phallus (?) or cucumber (?) (Manchester University Museum 1792)
8   ⌂ -shaped piece of ivory, to fit on the end of a stick (Manchester University Museum 1834)
9   Wooden paddle doll (Manchester University Museum 1832)
10   Limestone female figurine (Manchester University Museum 1789)
11   Blue faience female figurine (Manchester University Museum 1787)
12   Magical or religious figure: a wooden female figure with a partly animal head, and movable arms holding two bronze snakes (Manchester University Museum 1790; Bruyère 1930:174 fig. 92; Hall 1914:203, pl. 34 [2]; Bosse-Griffiths 1977:102–3 fig. 2; David 1982:pl. 9; Bourriau 1988:111 fig. 1)
13   Limestone female figurine (Manchester University Museum 1794)
14   Faience ape (Manchester University Museum 1835)
15   Ivory *djed* (Manchester University Museum 1838)
16   Faience lotus-shaped cup (Manchester University Museum 1791)
17   Ivory hand-shaped clappers (Manchester University Museum 1796, 1797)
18   Fragments of an ivory magic rod (?) with incised figures of two lions (Manchester

University Museum 1795; for this identification see exx. of Bourriau 1988:115
[nos. 103–4])

19   Limestone female figurine (not illustrated by Quibell 1898)
20   Ivory figure of a dwarf(?) carrying a calf (unnumbered by Quibell 1898:pl. 2
        [1–2]); possibly of later date

While some of these are funerary items, the others have led to the suggestion that
the owner was a 'magician and medical practitioner' (G 1955a:1; followed by
Simpson 1972:66; Bourriau 1988:110), or more specifically a lector priest (Yoyotte
1957:174–5; Helck 1982b:726). Damaged during excavation, R was stored in
University College, London, until 1906, when it was transferred to Berlin for
treatment by Hugo Ibscher (G 1955a:2–3; VG:5); the identification of the text was
published the following year (G 1907:1–2). The unrolled papyrus (recto) was
published with photographs and transcription in 1908 by Vogelsang and Gardiner.
It is now in the Staatliche Museen, Berlin, together with two unpublished fragments
(see 1.3).

1.3   DESCRIPTION

The conventions used here are taken in part from Turner 1978:§7 and passim,
including 'kollesis' to mean the terminal edge of a sheet overlapping the next sheet
('7.7 K ^{1}' means 'from the right 7.7. cm, then first kollesis'). The terms 'recto' and
'verso' are retained here, designating the inside and outside of the roll, with
horizontal and vertical fibres, respectively (Turner 1978:§3.2).

P Berlin 3023 (B1)

Dimensions: 390 × 16 cm. Like the other Berlin manuscripts it is a halved roll
(Černý 1952:15; Helck 1974:8). For the dimensions of the individual Amherst
fragments see Newberry 1899:17.

Colour: Dark brown. It is discoloured on the second page of the verso, which is
generally yellower.

Texture: There are traces of palimpsest on the recto, particularly clear along the top
edge (see fig. 4). These can be observed at the following points: B1 21–2, 25–7, 32–8
a horizontal rubric, 55–6, 59, 66, 74–5 a vertical rubric, 75, 76, 79–81, 81–6 a
horizontal rubric, 85–6, 96, 104, 122, 133, 136 a horizontal rubric, 153, 180, 196,
216–7, 255, 256, 271, 278–9. On the verso there are traces above B1 316 (in general,
see Caminos 1986). The surface of the verso is more damaged and uneven, due at
least partly to its being more extensively palimpsest. In places it is now very thin and
transparent.

Kolleseis (vertical):   7.7 K^1 (incomplete sheet); 49 K^2; 35.6 K^3; 51.1 K^4; 33 K^5; 54.5
K^6; 54.2 K^7; 51.4 K^8; 53.3 K^9. The kolleseis are right over left on the recto, except

for K³, and possibly K⁴ (uncertain due to mounting). K⁵ has been reinforced by a
strip of papyrus (1.0–1.2 cm wide) on the recto.

Preservation: There are 326 lines on the Berlin manuscript with a further 29 and
fragments of a column of a list on P Amherst I. As these can be joined exactly (see
fig. 1), the lines are here renumbered, and the whole designated B1. A concordance
of old and new numbers is provided in 1.8. The text of R suggests that some 12
lines must now be missing from the start.

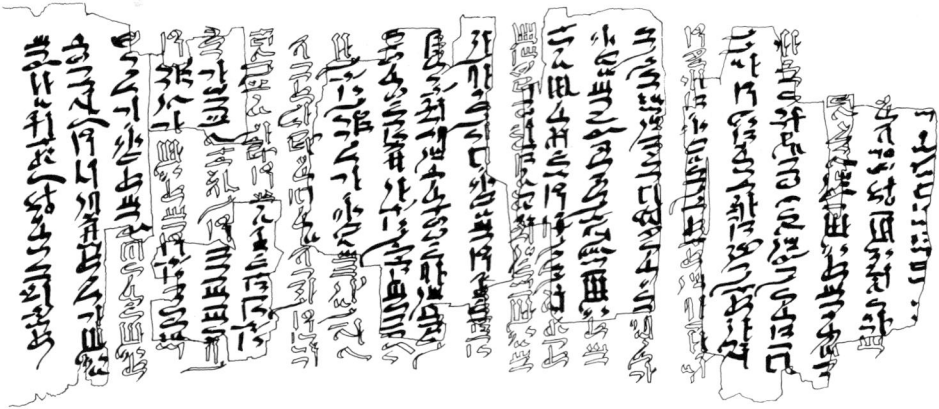

Figure 1   A restoration of the beginning of B1 (0.33 : 1; after Möller 1927b: 13–14)

Format: On the recto there are traces of six horizontal ruled guidelines (for this term
see Tait 1986:77–8 n.2), c.3.2 cm apart; these are sometimes very clear but
elsewhere erased; the verso has less extensive traces of these lines (see fig. 4). Similar
guidelines are also found on P Berlin 3024 (*Lebensmüder*) and on the verso of R.
They were intended to facilitate the alignment of corresponding entries in accounts
and ledgers arrranged in widely spaced columns (Hayes 1955:8–9; Simpson
1963:18–19, nn. 13–14; Helck 1974:47–8; Megally 1977:3; Tait 1986). The single
vertical line (through 134–45) may be similarly explained (e.g. Simpson 1963:19
n.14). Commenting on P Brooklyn 35.1446 (verso), Hayes suggested that such
guidelines had largely fallen out of use by the mid 13th dynasty (1955:9; see also
Helck 1974:48). When they were used primarily to format a literary text, only the
equivalents of the top and bottom guidelines were ruled (e.g. P Ram. D: G 1947:8;
Tait 1986:72, 83 n.64), but this is not the case here. The top guideline is the same
distance from the top edge as on P Berlin 3024 (*Lebensmüder*) and on R. The clean
ends of the guidelines at the present end of the manuscript show that it was the same
length when prepared for accounts as now. The reinforcement of K⁵ was made

before the guidelines were drawn. The partial erasure of the guidelines on the recto
and verso suggests that an unevenly distributed text (or texts) was partially written
over the roll; the roll was then halved and the text erased, carelessly along the top
edge. Few of the palimpsest traces are legible; at B1 21-2 *dd.hr=k* is clear, and at B1
25 *gm=k*. These forms are suggestive of a medical text, while other traces are
compatible with accounts (B1 271; 278–9). This reuse is similar to that of P Berlin
3024 (*Lebensmüder*), which has less extensive traces of similar guidelines and clearer
traces of the text of the accounts (G 1909:6; Goedicke 1970:1, n.5). The verso of
B1 also was prepared and used, perhaps secondarily (Helck 1974:47), before the
Tale was written.

Lines 1–285 of the Tale are on the recto, beginning where the goods carried by
the peasant are listed (B1 1–14). The list of goods was arranged in one and a sixth
vertical columns of horizontal items, with the determinatives forming sub-columns.
B1 15–16 are written beneath the one-sixth column. Traces of line-numbering were
thought to exist above B1 56 and 66, reading 60 and 70 respectively, but these are
probably palimpsest:

B1 56   B1 66

Figure 2   The traces above B1 56, 66 (0.9:1)

The arrangement of the Tale is shown in fig. 3; the columns written in horizontal
lines may reflect the scribe's concern when writing the middle portion to fit the text
on the papyrus (compare the similar arrangement of P Berlin 3022 [*Sinuhe*]). The
writing is more spacious for the final few lines of the recto, and after B1 285 there is
a blank space of 7.5 cm, occupying the remainder of the recto, enough for three
further lines. The roll was then turned on a horizontal axis, and the text begins on
the verso at a spot equivalent to B1 152 on the recto. The preceding portions of the
roll may have been left blank because the surface was damaged (it is no longer
visible due to mounting). The second column of horizontal lines on the verso,
which begins with the start of the peasant's seventh petition, is left short, to avoid
writing on traces of erased text (previously unread); after B1 304 the scribe wrote
two lines of text which occur later (B1 310–12); he realised his mistake, and erased
them before writing B1 305. The blot beneath these lines may have been caused by
putting his pen down while making the erasure. I include a facsimile, with
restoration and transcription: (fig. 4, p. xviii).

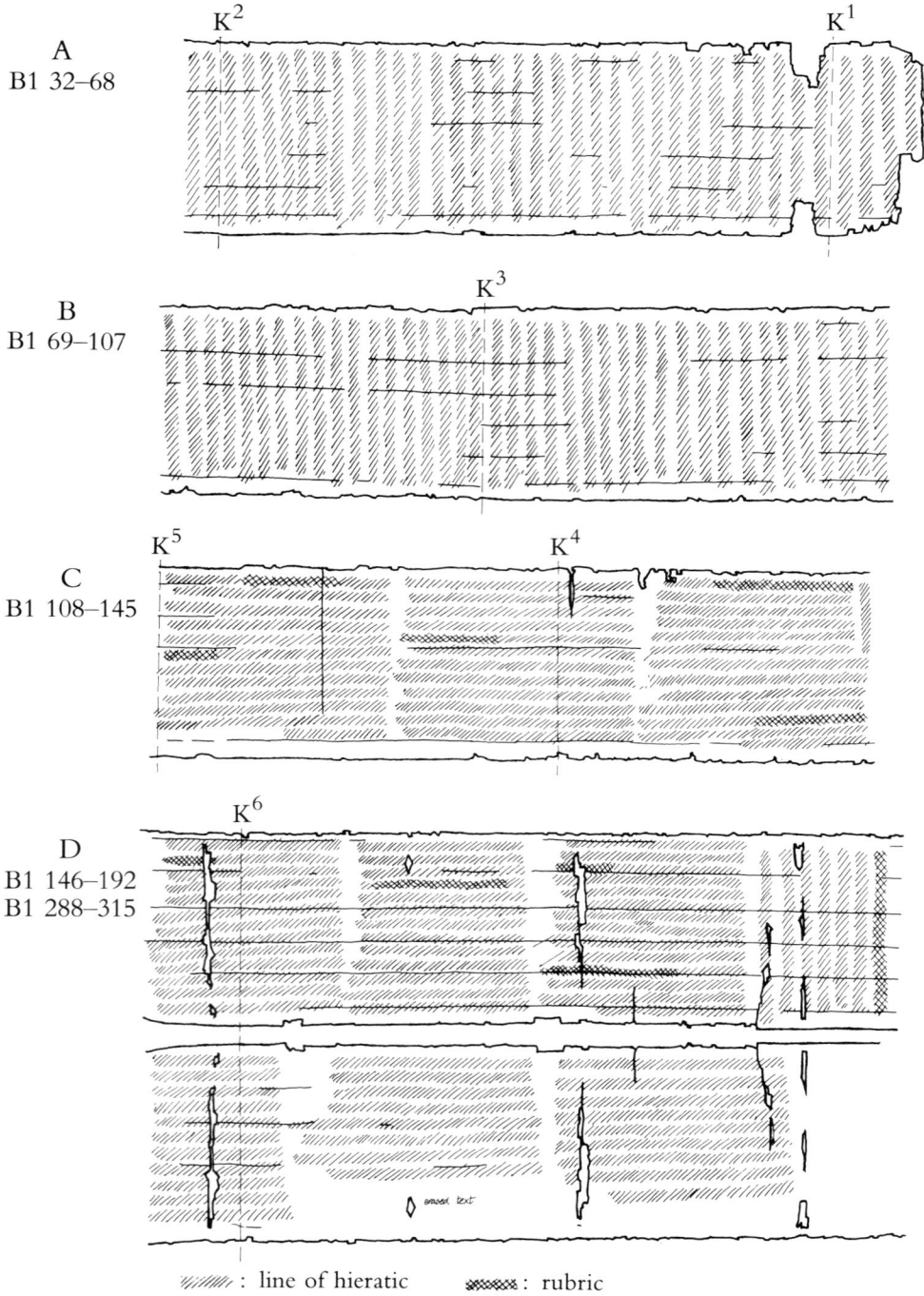

A
B1 32–68

B
B1 69–107

C
B1 108–145

D
B1 146–192
B1 288–315

: line of hieratic   : rubric

Figure 3   Diagram of the arrangement of B1 on recto and verso (0.17 : 1)

E
B1 193–237
B1 305–335

K^7

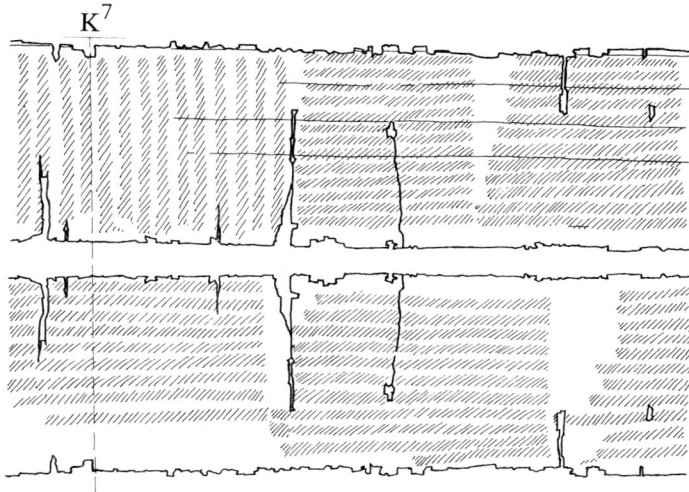

F
B1 231–260
B1 327–357

K^8

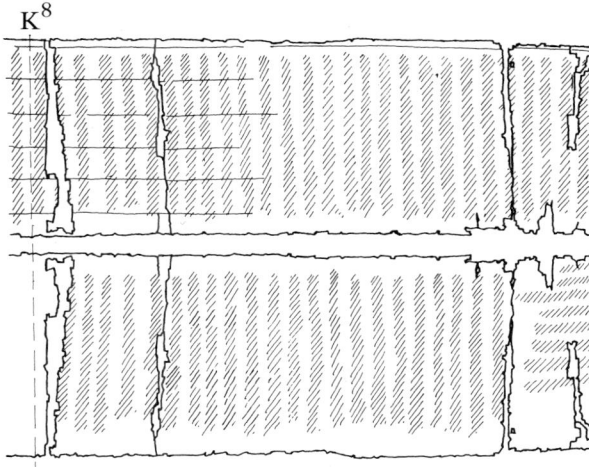

G
B1 261–287

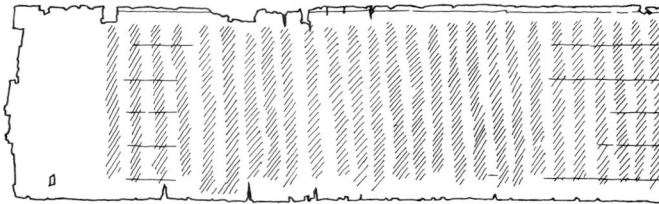

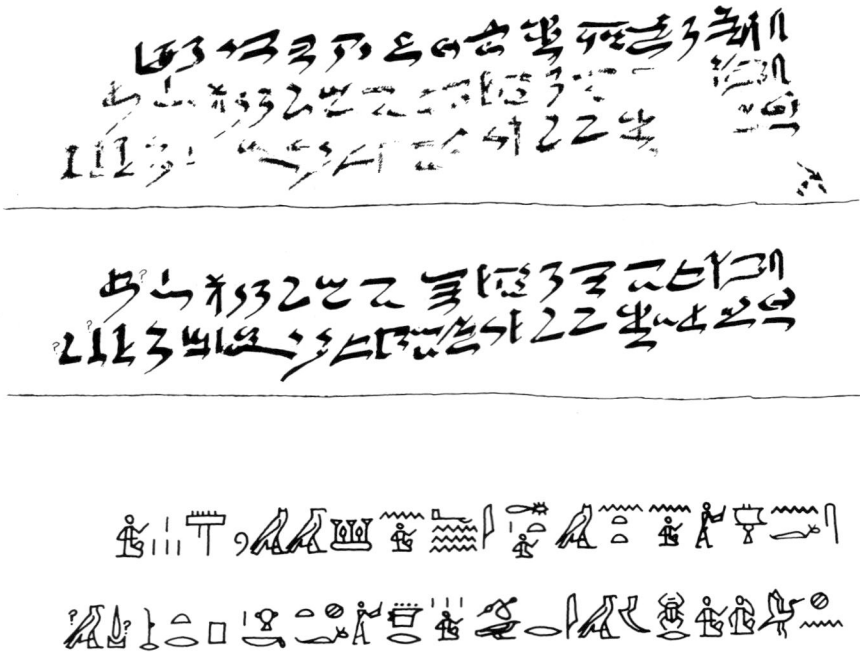

Figure 4   The erased lines of B1 (0.49 : 1)

The fifth column is slightly short, although the surface beneath is not noticeably damaged. B1 verso ends with the conclusion of the eighth petition at a point equivalent to B1 258 on the recto. There would not have been enough room to include the ninth petition or the concluding narrative on the roll, and thus a second manuscript was necessary for the owner of the 'library' of Berlin manuscripts to possess the whole Tale (see 1.2).

Hand: Black ink is used, with rubrics only in the first six columns of horizontal lines on the recto and at B1 146 – the only vertical example (cf. Assmann 1983:41 on the irregular rubrics of P Berlin 3022 [*Sinuhe*]). Allowing for the differing surfaces, the pen thickness is probably the same on recto and verso: c. 2–2.5 mm; the number of signs written with a single dipping increases on the verso. The hand itself is accomplished and regular in the vertical lines; when horizontal it is more cursive (e.g. ⌘ and ⌘ in 106 and 113) and much less elegantly arranged, especially towards the end of the recto and on the verso, and uses more ligatures. On the verso it is generally more cursive, and appears more hurried. The inferior surface explains this at least partially. The full forms of 𓄿, 𓄿, 𓅱, and 𓀀 are found quite frequently; as their use is dictated by space and by word grouping, they are more frequent in vertical lines. Vogelsang and Gardiner noted that the scribe 'scheut ... nicht vor Ligaturen .... Große Mühe macht oft die Unterscheidung von ⟨⟩, ⟨⟩ und ⟨⟩ auch sonst sind die einzelnen Formen der Zeichen so verschieden gemacht oder entstellt, daß die Lesung keineswegs zu den leichtesten Aufgaben gezählt werden kann' (6). The hand is the same as that of P Berlin 3022 (*Sinuhe*; see further G 1909:4–5). Corrections or deletions of errors are found in B1 134(?), 140(?), 153(?), 154, 230(?), 336, 342; these can be confused with traces of palimpsest. The scribe apparently became less careful towards the end of the verso (e.g. B1 345, 348), though some uncorrected errors are found earlier (e.g. B1 273). It seems that the corrections and deletions of mistakes – no less obvious than the uncorrected mistakes – were made in the course of writing.

P Berlin 3025 (B2)

Dimensions: 295 × 15 cm, a halved roll.

Colour: Darker than B1, and the sheets are less even in tone.

Texture: Coarser and less even than B1. There are slight indications of palimpsest (e.g. between 102–3, 106–7), but any previous text was well erased. Not very transparent.

Kolleseis: 27.5 K[1] (incomplete); 45.6 K[2]; 44.9 K[3]; 46.7 K[4]; 45.4 K[5]; 48.7 K[6]; 34.9 K[7]. They are right over left on the recto.

Preservation: The papyrus appears more fragmented than B1, with more severe vertical cracking. The fragments were misarranged by Lepsius (*LD* VI, 113–14) thus: his '1–3' are B2 133–5; '4–10', 126–32; '11–17',136–42; '18–142', 1–125. The end becomes increasingly damaged and missing at the bottom, and it is uncertain how much is lost at the beginning and end; the roll need not have contained the whole text. 142 lines survive in the Berlin sections, and parts of another four in P Amherst II, fragments F and G. The relationship of the fragments is shown in fig. 5 (p. xx). As the joins are not direct and the exact number of vertical lines lost between G and F is uncertain, I have not included their lines in my numbering.

Format: The text occupies the recto, written vertically. The lines are evenly spaced, slightly more widely at the start and on the final sheet. The verso is bare apart from a small area of writing, equivalent to B2 54–6 on the recto. The facsimile of the surviving traces included here (fig. 6) has been collated with *LD* VI, 114, in which the signs are less fragmentary, although still illegible. Its position in the middle of the roll shows that it cannot have been a roll-label or title, but was probably a scribal jotting (cf. P Ram. I [*The Discourse of Sisobek*] verso: Barns 1956: pl. 25).

Figure 5   A restoration of the beginning of B2 (0.35 : 1)

Figure 6   The verso of B2, with a copy of *LD* VI, 114 (0.9 : 1)

Hand: There are three rubrics (B2 21, 50, 91, all *jw.jn-rf*). The pen thickness is
c. 1.5–2.0 mm; the ink flow is less regular than in B1. The hand itself is very similar
to that of B1, but much less careful (e.g. *mk* in B1 344 and B2 78:). A
comparison of B2 71–9 with the vertical B1 336–57 reveals why Vogelsang and

Gardiner (6) considered that they might be the work of the same scribe, but Möller's contrary view is confirmed, not only by particular signs (e.g. 🕭 (M. 594): B1 𝄢 , B2 𝄡) but also by the spacing of words and the more spacious arrangement of lines (1927a : 15). The absence of the fully written 🦅 is also relevant. The text is corrected, notably in 82 and 100 (?). The former contains a gap of 3–4 groups, due either to palimpsest traces making the surface unusable, or to an error purposely expunged.

P Butler

Dimensions: 72 × 13.7 cm. The edges have been trimmed in modern times, but suggest an original height of c. 15 cm.

Colour: A light brown; yellower on verso.

Texture: The recto shows palimpsest traces of a text written in horizontal lines with a number of short rubrics (Bt 7, 18–9, 21, 24, 28, 29–30, 32); it has been thoroughly cleaned and the traces are illegible. The surface is more extensively damaged on the verso, and it is unclear if this is also palimpsest. Very thin and transparent.

Kolleseis: One is preserved at Bt (recto) 28–9, 44.5 K^1. It is right over left (recto).

Preservation: The unfortunate mounted state of the papyrus was described by Griffith (1892 : 458); this has recently been remedied. 40 lines are preserved on the recto.

Format: The text of the Tale occupies the recto, beginning with the list of the peasant's goods. This is arranged as in B1, though the first column has eleven horizontal items and the second three; the determinatives form a separate sub-column. Bt 15–16 are long vertical lines, cramped beneath Bt 12–14. Griffith detected traces of line numbers, which could be read 20 and 30, although partially cut away (1892 : 459–61):

Bt 19   Bt 29

Figure 7   The supposed line numbers above Bt recto 19, 29 (0.9 : 1); after Griffith 1892

Both the traces are now lost; that above Bt 19 was on a fragment which may well have been misplaced (so Gunn MS), but the other trace was certain. However, this was probably a palimpsest trace, similar to that above Bt 29–30. There is a dash above Bt 16, which Griffith related to the principle of numbering (1892 : 460); it is doubtful whether his analysis is correct. The amount of text lost at the start, to judge by that preserved in R, would require another at least 20 cm of papyrus, suggesting a previous sheet must be lost at the beginning of the roll, unless the one on which the text now begins was unusually long.

The roll was turned about on a horizontal axis to write the verso text, whose numbering is much clearer (Möller 1927a : 8):

Bt verso 12   Bt verso 22   Bt verso 32

Figure 8   The line numbers above Bt verso 12, 22, 32 (0.9 : 1)

These figures show that eight lines are lost, suggesting a wider initial border than on the recto. The text is written in what Gunn called 'the most difficult hieratic ... of the M[iddle] K[ingdom]' (letter to Blackman, 4.10.1938, in B II). This difficulty is due to the cursiveness of the hand as well as the damaged surface and flaked ink, and it has hindered study of the text. In addition to Griffith's published transcription, there is a set of notes by Gunn (MS), and a transcription by Blackman (in B II). The text is distinct from the Tale, but is a discourse (Posener 1951a : 34 no. 12), apparently involving a similar pleader. The setting is pastoral: mention is made of the goddess *Sḫt* and of the countryside. Posener suggested that it is part of the text whose title is elsewhere preserved as 'the discourse of a fowler of the Southern City, Iuru' (1969 : 103, 105–6).

Hand: There is only one sign in red, Bt (recto) 14, probably a later correction. The pen thickness is c. 1–1.5 mm, and the number of signs written with a single dipping is very variable. The writing is larger and swifter on the verso, at least partially due to the surface; although the hands look dissimilar in places, they could well be the same. The hand of the recto itself is of the same style as the Berlin manuscripts and very similar to that of B2, although it uses the full forms of ⟨glyph⟩, ⟨glyph⟩, ⟨glyph⟩, and ⟨glyph⟩ (see 1.2, 1.4), and forms ⟨glyph⟩, ⟨glyph⟩ quite differently. The pen thickness is 1–1.5 mm (recto). In Bt (recto) 3 and 14 there are corrections probably made while writing.

P Ramesseum A

Dimensions: The major part is 240 cm long, as mounted; of the other main fragments which were known before 1908, I–II are quite small, 3.4 × 2.5 and 3.0 × 2.2 cm, and III is 20 cm long (VG : 5; G 1909 : 1). If these fragments are added to the major part, with the lost portions, the papyrus would be 4.25m long (G 1909:1). It is 8.2 cm high, a quartered roll, which occurs with four literary texts in the Middle Kingdom (Černý 1952:15; Helck 1974:8).

Colour: Yellow-brown, in places quite dark (VG:5), due to (modern) damp (G 1955a:7).

Texture: Of very high quality (VG:5). The text is palimpsest, most obviously under column 1, where there are traces of rubrics. Very thin but not transparent.

Kolleseis: The major fragment is of six sheets, of which five are relatively complete: 34.6 K^1; 44.3 K^2; 46.4 K^3; 33.5 K^4; 39.5 K^5. The kolleseis on the recto are right over left.

Preservation: Quibell found it in 'extremely bad condition' (1898:3), and it is now very fragmentary with large areas completely lost, perhaps due to its being dropped on discovery and to its subsequent treatment (a rumour recounted by G 1955a:7). The start of the text is less fragmentary, having been originally at the centre of the roll. The identification of further fragments during 1908 led Vogelsang and Gardiner to add extra plates to their publication (4 bis, 4 bis a; described: G 1909:1 – the fragments are unnumbered). In 1912 more fragments were found, one of which (R 19.4–7) was published in transcription (G 1923:22); the other 'somewhat larger' piece (R 20.2–7) remained unpublished, being 'without noteworthy variants' (G 1955a:7–8). Facsimiles of these are included here (fig. 9, p.xxiv).

The aggregate of the pieces of R amounts to the remains of 229 lines on the recto, while the text of *Sinuhe* on the verso has 203 lines (G 1909:pl.4 bis). The major part, including fragments I–II, contains R 1.1–20.7. A 1908 fragment comprises R 23.1–24.7, III contains R 25.1–27.8, and another 1908 fragment R 30.6–31.8.

Format: A margin of 2.5 cm is left blank at the start of the recto. The text is arranged in columns of horizontal lines, which are here renumbered in accordance with this pagination; a concordance is given in 1.8.

After the first column of seven long lines comes the list of the peasant's goods, arranged in four narrow vertical columns of horizontal items. Three columns contain seven items each, the fourth six written more spaciously. The determinatives form subcolumns, aligned with the longest item in the column (2–5). Columns 6–8 are of seven lines each; a single vertical line follows, written thus to allow column 9 to start with a rubric. Columns 9–11 are of seven lines, 12 of eight with a short last line. 13 has eight long lines, followed by two vertical lines, written thus for the same reason as 8.8. Columns 14–15 have seven lines, 16 eight (the extra line may relate to one of the petitions ending in the middle of R 13.8), 17–20 seven. 21–22, which are completely lost, were probably of seven lines each (so VG pl.4 bis). Columns 23–24 have seven lines, 25–7 eight; the lines of 26 are rather short,

27.1 being rubricized. 28–9 are completely lost. Of 30, the ends of lines 6–7 survive; Vogelsang and Gardiner assumed a short eighth line, but this is unlikely (pl. 4 bis). 31 has eight lines, the first of which is lost.

On the verso, the roll having been turned on a horizontal axis, *Sinuhe* begins after a margin of 11 cm. It is formatted into 30 columns of horizontal lines, of which four are completely lost. There are traces of three horizontal ruled guidelines from column 25 (= R 133) on (see above for these).

Hand: Rubrics are frequent throughout, marking the start of speeches and petitions, regardless of the metrical scheme. The pen thickness is c. 1–2 mm. A single dipping seems to write a whole line, the scribe redipping at the end of each line before the ink ran out; because of this inking method the blackness is very even. The hand itself is 'eine schöne literarische Hand, die sowohl in den Zeichenformen wie in der Orthographie äußerst konsequent ist. Die größeren Nebenformen ... sind wohl wegen des kleinen Formats im allgemeinen vermieden, doch kommen sie bei 🐦 und 🏛 in der vertikalen [R 8.8], wie auch bei 🦅 in der vertikalen [R 13.10] sowie in der Liste [R 5.1] vor' (VG: 5). The last of these is a widely spaced column. The hand is generally neater than the horizontal part of B1 and B2 and the lines are more elegantly arranged. The forms are more angular, due partly to a sharper pen and the small size of the signs (see also 1.4). Corrections and deletions made while writing are found (e.g. 13.4 and 25.6).

The hand of the verso (*Sinuhe*) is less careful and hastier than that of the recto, but is certainly of the same scribe (G 1909: 4).

Figure 9   The unpublished fragments of R (0.9:1)

I.4

DATING

P Berlin 3023 (B1) and 3025 (B2)

Möller (1927a : 15) considered these to be contemporaneous, and there is contextual evidence for this assumption (see 1.2, 1.3). B2 is generally more cursive, and, though there are not many major variations betwen the hands of the manuscripts, some signs may suggest a marginally later date than B1 : [hieroglyph] (M. 207b) is as in R ([hieroglyph]), not as in B1 ([hieroglyph]); [hieroglyph] (M. 582) is also as in R ([hieroglyph]), not B1 ([hieroglyph]). These differences may not be significant as a dating criterion, and should not override the general similarity. The textual variants of the two relate primarily to the difference between the manuscripts' textual archetypes and not directly to the date of their writings.

The Berlin manuscipts are generally accepted to date 'to the very end of the 12th. or to the beginning of the 13th. Dynasty' (G 1916 : 2); of these, P Berlin 3022 (*Sinuhe*) cannot predate the reign of Sesostris I. Möller concurred (1927a : 15), comparing this group with Papyri Kahun (Illahun) and P Bulaq 18 (year 3 of Sobekhotpe II, early 13th dynasty: cf. Spalinger 1984 : 1038, n. 12). However, the evolution presented in Möller's tables is vitiated by his misplacing of P Prisse before the Berlin group, not after (he later recognized this: Dévaud 1924 : i–ii, n. 5). Only the hands of other similar literary texts can be used for comparative dating, since different forms characterize different types of manuscripts as well as stages in evolution, which need not be contemporaneous in different types. For this period, the relevant datable manuscripts are P Kahun LV.1, VI.12, which are from the first group of Illahun papyri, dating from Amenemhat III and his successors (Simpson 1974 : 67; see also Möller 1927a : 13; Matzker 1986 : 116–21). These are *Hymns to Sesostris III, The Tale of Hay*, and a narrative concerning Horus and Seth (Griffith 1898 : pl. 1–4). Of these, the first cannot predate Sesostris III, and may have been roughly contemporaneous with his reign (so Posener 1956 : 128). The hands of B1 and B2 appear generally similar to these, but not exactly. Some signs link them with later manuscripts; thus, for [hieroglyph] (M. 200) Illahun has only [hieroglyph] , while B1/2 has also [hieroglyph] and Bulaq 18 [hieroglyph] . Similarly for [hieroglyph] (M. 237) Illahun and earlier texts have [hieroglyph] , B1/2, Prisse and Bulaq 18 [hieroglyph] . For [hieroglyph] (M. 393) Illahun has [hieroglyph] , B1/2 and later (Hyksos period) [hieroglyph] . However, such differences may relate more to such factors as regional variation than to date.

Similar reservations affect Dévaud's analysis of orthography (1924) and Berlev's remarks on the date of the Tale (1987 : 83). Dévaud's analysis, in general, links the Berlin group to the 12th dynasty Illahun papyri and separates them from those of the 13th dynasty. Of the words selected by him, only two show an orthography in

B1/2 different from that found in the 12th dynasty Illahun manuscripts (nos. 5: *dbꜣw*, 7: *ꜥḥꜣ*); in these cases the Illahun manuscripts have forms found in later manuscripts, although for no. 7 they also have the form found in the Berlin group. This distribution suggests that the Berlin manuscripts may have been written earlier, rather than later, than some of the Illahun group, and strengthens the general impression that the Berlin manuscripts are closer to 12th dynasty examples than to those of the 13th. Berlev observes that *wr* 'chief' (as in *jmjrꜣ pr-wr*, e.g. B1 20) is first attested as 𓀀 in hieratic (and hieroglyphs) under Amenemhat III (in the Semna Despatches; 1987:83). The ruled horizontal guidelines are a further pointer to this date, being rare by the mid 13th dynasty (Hayes 1955:9), although their absence in B2 need not be significant in this context.

Thus these two manuscripts are probably to be dated to the end of the 12th dynasty, not long after the reigns of Sesostris III and Amenemhat III. The two are closely contemporaneous, though B2 may be marginally later.

P Butler

Vogelsang and Gardiner (7) and Möller (1927a:15) agreed that Bt and the Berlin manuscripts come from the same period. Gardiner suggested that it is 'perhaps roughly contemporary' with P Ram. D (Onomasticon), which also has numbered lines (1947:7 n. 1). The sampling of the hand is too small for firm conclusions, but it is almost identical to B2 (see 1.3), although in style it appears more careful, fine and angular, like B1's (if less neat). As in B2, some signs are closer to the forms in R than to those in B1: 𓅆 (M. 207b) is as in B2 and R (⚓), not B1 (⚓); 𓏏𓏏𓏏 (M. 504) is as in R (⚓), P Berlin 3024 (*Lebensmüder*), Illahun, Bulaq 18, not B1 (⚓); ⎣ (M. 584) is as in R and B2 (⟋) not B1 (⚓). None of Dévaud's selected words appears in a revealing variant.

These factors suggest a date similar to B2, marginally later than B1.

P Ramesseum A

R is the only manuscript which has a potentially datable context. Of the objects from the tomb, the ivory wands have been dated by H. Altenmüller (1965). Numbers 1, 2a and 2b are of his type IV (*ibid.* I, 59, II, 108–10, 118), another example of which is incorporated in a pectoral with the name of Sesostris III (*ibid.* I, 77–8); type IV is thus to be dated to around his reign. 3 is less typologically clear, but has been dated stylistically to several decades later (*ibid.* II, 111). All are characteristic of the late 12th dynasty, as opposed to the 13th, when a new type is found (*ibid.* I, 78). These suggest a *terminus post quem* for the burial in the late 12th dynasty.

Some of the Ramesseum papyri can be dated by content. The Semna Despatches (C) are copies of administrative memoranda which were dated on internal evidence by Smither to the reign of Amenemhat III (1945:5), although Spanel does not accept this as conclusive (1984:844 nn.4–5). The Onomasticon (D) contains a place name *sꜣ* [*rꜥ*] *jmn-m-ḥꜣt mꜣꜥ-ḥrw ꜥꜣ-bꜣw* (l.210; G 1947:pl.2a), and so probably postdates Amenemhat III. The hymns to Sobek of Shedyt (VI) mention an Amenemhat without *mꜣꜥ-ḥrw*, and thus were perhaps composed, if not written down in this manuscript, under Amenemhat III, or possibly IV (G 1957=44). Stylistically, many of these papyri can be considered roughly contemporary with the Berlin group. The literary *Discourse of Sisobek* (I) is strikingly similar in style and format to the Berlin group. P. Ramesseum II (recto), III (verso), XI and XII have horizontal ruled guidelines, supporting a date before the mid 13th dynasty (see 1.3). However, others (e.g. XVI) show flourishes suggestive of the mid to late 13th dynasty (see Megally 1971:5). The papyri are as varied in style and date as in content, although Gardiner estimated that they probably do not range 'over a greater period than about a century' (1947:6; cf. G 1955a:2). These factors provide a *terminus post quem* for the tomb in the mid 13th dynasty.

R's hand is distinct from the B group, perhaps because it is the work of a fine calligrapher, as noted by Megally (1971:4 n.2). This, however, can be no more than a partial explanation. Megally analyses the hand as presenting 'moins de traits penchés horizontaux ou verticaux, moins d'angles aigus, une préférence pour des formes pleines dont les détails ont des proportions et une disposition plus proches de celles des détails des formes hiéroglyphiques [referring to VG:pl.53a], et enfin moins de ligatures'(1971:4). Gardiner considered some signs to recall the Hyksos group: ⸗ (M.167), ⸗ (M.284), ⸗ (M.374), ⸗ (M.223), ⸗ (M.279, examples with side dash). Others recall the Berlin manuscripts: ⸗ (M.381) and ⸗ (M.379, with a high side dash), ⸗ (M.508, without the dot above), ⸗ (M.205, with the legs as a single stroke). ⸗ (M.16) is characteristic, being distinct from the B group, but not yet 'disintegrated, as in the Ebers, into two distinct signs' (1916:2–3). It is, however, free from the 'flourishes' of the Hyksos group. G's final placing – after the Berlin group and before P Bulaq 18 (i.e. year 3 of Sobekhotpe II, the early 13th dynasty: 1947:6) – was in agreement with Möller, who considered it to be closer to the former (1927a:16). Megally sees R as characteristic of 13th dynasty hieratic, which develops the tendencies of the 12th dynasty, but also reveals 'un développement graphique plutôt dans le sens inverse, visant à rendre moins abrégées, moins codées, voire plus complètes, les formes' (1971:3). Dévaud's analysis of orthography led him to assign R to the 13th dynasty (1924). There are horizontal ruled guidelines on the verso, which may argue against placing R late in that dynasty (see 1.3).

Thus, the Ramesseum burial can be dated to the mid to late 13th dynasty, with R being written early in the dynasty. A more precise estimate of the period between its writing and B1 and B2 cannot be given.

1.5 THE RELATIONSHIPS OF THE MANUSCRIPTS

Although the Tale is almost unique in the number of its preserved Middle Kingdom manuscripts, they are insufficient in quantity and in providing parallel texts for a full stemmatisation of the textual transmission: only for B1 1–34 are there more than two manuscripts. The following description of the relationship of the manuscripts adopts the guidelines and terminology of Maas (1958), as does Schenkel (1978; see also Blumenthal 1983 : 236–7, whose reservations are excessive).

B1 and Bt always agree against R, save in B1 24, 25 27, 33 (V : 2–3). Some of these minor variants are not 'indicative', and cannot be considered 'conjunctive errors' (Maas 1958 : 43) allying Bt and R to the same textual tradition, since Bt's variants against B1 are probably due to error in B1's tradition (which the scribe of Bt could have removed by conjecture). The variants of R against B1 can be considered 'separative errors' (Maas 1958 : 42), revealing that R is not merely a later development of B1's textual tradition (although many of the variants can be thus dismissed: V : 3–4), but represents an independent tradition. The extent of R's 'redactional' variants supports this analysis (B1 109–18 = R 17.6–19.6).

The position of B2 in any stemmatisation is very uncertain, as there are 250 possible stemma types with 4 textual witnesses (Maas 1958 : 47). Provenance and date ally it with B1, but the same factors indicate that its variants against B1 must be separative. B2 varies against B1 more frequently than the roughly contemporary Bt (although there are no fully parallel passages), which suggests that it is not from the same tradition. B2 also probably belongs to a separate tradition from R; B2 lacks both R's tendency to interpolate from elsewhere in the text (R 16.5–8, 26.4–6) and its redactional variants against B1 (see above).

B1 contains many minor errors and miswritings, and although B2 shows signs of corrections, it too has a substantial number of similar errors (see 1.3). On the whole, Bt is the most carefully written manuscript (see summary of V : 8–9), but these facts do not necessarily reflect the quality of the textual traditions represented. Many variants are inexplicable merely as errors of hearing or reading, and while some of them may have been induced by memory, others reflect a more deliberate redactional activity (cf. Burkard 1977). It is difficult to decide which manuscript variants are preferable as a whole, or to proclaim any one stemma superior to the others; as Gardiner concluded of *Sinuhe*, 'all variants must be examined and judged on their [individual] merits' (1916 : 163). Nevertheless, it seems that R contains the largest number of readings which can be explained as redactional alterations, although it may preserve some archetypal readings lost in B1 (this contrasts with the textual tranmission of *Sinuhe*, where R is often better than B, though also more evolved). The metrical structure and the character of the list of the peasant's goods (B1 1–14 = R 2.1–5.6) favours B1 as superior there, a conclusion probably valid for B1 and R as wholes (also, R contains two irregular 4-cola lines, as opposed to only one in B1: Fecht 1982 : 1140). Preference for a shorter version, which is also a principle of biblical textual tradition (Tigay 1985 : 8), favours B1 against R.

It is more difficult to judge between B1 and B2. V considered B2 superior, with the variations in length being the result of B1's tendency to omit phrases in copying, which he compared with its occasional omission of individual radicals (6–7). While B2 is a more carefully corrected manuscript, the parallel of R shows that a shorter version may be preferable. The relationships of B2 to B1 and R to B1 are different in nature, as is shown by the fact that B2's number of omissions against B1 is smaller than R's; B2 provides many variants of equivalence. Thus the following stemmatisation can be suggested:

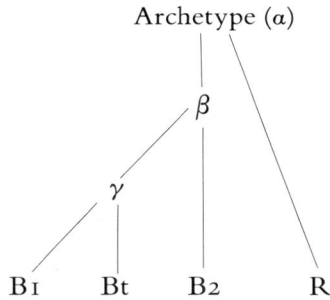

Archetype (α)

β

γ

B1   Bt   B2   R

The textual transmission is compatible with a composition date for the archetype in the middle of the 12th dynasty (Berlev 1987; Parkinson 1988; Vernus 1990).

The textual transmission of the Tale has often been assumed to end with the 13th dynasty (e.g. Baines 1982 : 32–3) – a sign than it had fallen out of favour (e.g. Erman 1923 : 157–8) after popularity in the Middle Kingdom, from which it is attested in as many surviving copies as *Sinuhe* (cf. Simpson 1984 : 952). However, contrary evidence is provided by *Menna's Instruction to his Son*, a literary ostracon of the reign of Ramesses IV from Deir el-Medineh (first noticed by G, 1923 : 25; published: Černý & Gardiner 1957 : pl. 78–9; translations and studies: Simpson 1958; Guglielmi 1983, Foster 1984, Sturtewagen *et al.* 1985; Goedicke 1987). Verso ll. 6–7 read:

You are in the situation of the one who said:
'You kill, my asses are taken
and complaint is seized from my mouth.'

This echoes B1 59–60; the specific nature of the final phrase suggests that the lines are an allusion to or loose quotation from the Tale (Guglielmi 1983 : 159, nn. z, aa; for a contrary translation and interpretation see Goedicke 1987 : 74 [54], 78).

The lack of actual New Kingdom manuscripts and ostraca may be due to chances of preservation or to the length and complexity of the Tale, which would make it unsuitable for use in scribal training – a major source of New Kingdom literary copies (the reservations of van der Plas, 1986 : 12–13, about this presumed provenance for ostraca are excessive).

1.6   PUBLICATIONS: A CHRONOLOGICAL SUMMARY

For publications up to 1908, articles relating to new readings of individual passages are listed; thereafter, only substantial transcriptions and corrections are included, later references to individual passages being incorporated in the textual notes.

1859   Lepsius, C. R., *Denkmaeler aus Aegypten und Aethiopien*, Abth. VI, pl. 108–10, 113–14. (Facsimiles of B1 and B2).

1863   Chabas, François, *Les Papyrus hiératiques de Berlin: récits d'il y a quatre mille ans, avec un index géographique et deux planches de fac-simile*. Chalon-sur-Saône: J. Dejussieu; reprinted in *Œuvres Diverses* II, 289–364, BÉ 10. Paris: Ernest Leroux 1902. (294–302 concern B1, with partial translation. General content is recognized, as is B2's relation to B1. Facsimile and full transcription of B1 170–76).

1864   Goodwin, Charles W., 'Lettre à F. Chabas sur un fragment hiératique se rattachant au Papyrus de Berlin No. II', in François Chabas, *Mélanges égyptologiques* IIe série, 249–66. (Partial transcription and translation of Bt, followed by a note by Chabas [266–72] with a revised transcription).

1864   Chabas, François, 'Sur un texte égyptien relatif au mouvement de la terre'. *ZÄS* 2, 97–103; reprinted in *Œuvres Diverses* III, 1–13, BÉ 11. Paris: Ernest Leroux 1903. (Transcription and study of B1 297–9).

1889   Borchardt, Ludwig, 'Bemerkungen zu den ägyptischen Handschriften des Berliner Museums'. *ZÄS* 27, 118–22. (Description of B1 and B2, also Bt, giving line numbers for the fragments).

1892   Griffith, Francis Ll., 'Fragments of Old Egyptian Stories from the British Museum and Amherst Collections'. *PSBA* 14, 451–72. (Facsimile by Newberry of Bt [pl. 1–4]; transcription, including B1; corrections to Lepsius' grouping of the B2 fragments).

1893   Müller, W. Max, 'The Story of the Peasant'. *PSBA* 15, 343–4. (A suggestion on Griffith's reading of 𓅯; also a note by the latter acknowledging two corrections to his transcription, = Bt 29, 37).

1894   Erman, Adolf, *Ägyptische Grammatik: mit Schrifttafel, Litteratur, Lesestücken und Wörterverzeichnis*; Lesestücke, 28*–37*. Porta Linguarum Orientalium 15. Berlin: Reuther & Reichard. (Transcription of Bt 16–33, B1 31–108).

1899   Newberry, Percy E., *The Amherst Papyri: being an account of the Egyptian Papyri in the Collection of the Right Hon. Lord Amherst of Hackney . . .* , 17–18, pl. 1. London: Bernard Quaritch. (Collotypes of A I and II, with a transcription of C and translation of the former).

1902–3 Schäfer, Heinrich, 'Eine kursive Form von 𓅯'. *ZÄS* 40, 121–4. (On the reading of 𓅯).

1904   Erman, Adolf, *Aegyptische Chrestomathie: zum Gebrauch auf Universitäten und zum Selbstunterricht*, 11–19, 6*–10*. Porta Linguarum Orientalium 19. Berlin: Reuther & Reichard. (Transcription and notes, as Erman 1894 : 28*–37*).

1904   Vogelsang, Friedrich, *Die Klagen des Bauern (aus Papyrus 3023 & 3025 der Königlichen Museen zu Berlin)*. Inaugural-Dissertation: Friedrich-Wilhelms-Universität zu Berlin. Berlin: Bernhard Paul. (First version of Vogelsang 1913. Transcription of B1 85–93, 119–28, 170–83, 218–20, 231–9, 252–6, 307–12 + B2 35–9, B1 319–20 + B2 48–50).

1908   Friedrich Vogelsang & Alan H. Gardiner, *Literarische Texte des Mittleren Reiches* IV: *Die Klagen des Bauern*. Hieratische Papyrus aus den Königlichen Museen zu Berlin 4. Leipzig: J. C. Hinrichs. (Publication of R, B1 (32 ff.) and B2 in photographs with transcription and translation).

1909   Möller, Georg, *Hieratische Lesestücke für den akademischen Gebrauch* I: *Alt- und mittelhieratische Texte*, pl. 12–16. Leipzig: J. C. Hinrichs. (Facsimile of R 1.1–8, B1 15–82).

1913   Vogelsang, Friedrich, *Kommentar zu den Klagen des Bauern*. UGAÄ 6.

1923   Gardiner, Alan H., 'The Eloquent Peasant'. *JEA* 9, 5–25. (Translation with corrections and additions to Vogelsang & Gardiner 1908).

1924   Sethe, Kurt, *Aegyptische Lesestücke zum Gebrauch im akademischen Unterricht: Texte des Mittleren Reiches*, 17–25. Leipzig: J. C. Hinrichs. (Partial transcription, omitting problematic passages).

1927   Möller, Georg, *Hieratische Lesestücke für den akademischen Gebrauch* I: *Alt- und mittelhieratische Texte*, pl. 12–16. 2nd edition. Leipzig: J. C. Hinrichs. (Revision of Möller 1909. Facsimile of R 1.1–8, B1 15–82).

1928   Sethe, Kurt, *Aegyptische Lesestücke zum Gebrauch im akademischen Unterricht: Texte des Mittleren Reiches*, 17–25. 2nd edition. Leipzig: J. C. Hinrichs. (Revision of Sethe 1924. Partial Transcription, omitting problematic passages).

1933   Suys, Émile, *Étude sur le conte du fellah plaideur: récit égyptien du Moyen-Empire*, 1*–31*. AnOr 5. Rome: Pontificio Istituto Biblico. (Transcription of the 'best' text with variants noted and innovations on previous readings; for evaluation see Blackman 1934).

1936–7? Aylward M. Blackman & H. W. Fairman, Fairman's transcript of Blackman's
transcription of all the mss (collated in late 1936: BI & II). (Complete parallel
text in pencil, inked as far as BI 67. Without textual notes, rough drafts for
which are in the notebooks. Intended to form *Middle Egyptian Stories*, 48–83;
Brussels: Fondation Égyptologique Reine Élisabeth. Now in School of Archaeology and Oriental Studies, University of Liverpool.)

1948   de Buck, Adriaan, *Egyptian Readingbook* I: *Exercises and Middle Egyptian Texts*,
88–99. Leiden: Nederlandsch Archaeologisch-Philologisch Instituut voor het
Nabije Oosten. (Partial transcription, omitting problematic passages; some
textual notes on p. 128).

1.7   ABBREVIATIONS AND REFERENCES

Discussions are referred to by name and date. Abbreviations not listed in Wolfgang Helck *et al.* (eds.), *Lexikon der Ägyptologie* VII (Wiesbaden: Otto Harrassowitz 1989–), are included here.

Altenmüller, Hartwig 1965, *Die Aptropaia und die Götter Mittelägyptens: eine typologische und religionsgeschichtliche Untersuchung der sogenannten "Zaubermesser" des Mittleren Reiches.* 2 vols. (Dissertation: Ludwig-Maximilians-Universität zu München).

Assmann, Jan 1983, 'Die Rubren in der Überlieferung der Sinuhe-Erzählung', in *Fontes atque Pontes: eine Festgabe für Hellmut Brunner*, Manfred Görg (ed.), 18–41. ÄUAT 5.

d'Athanasi, Giovanni 1836, *A Brief Account of the Researches and Discoveries in Upper Egypt, made under the direction of Henry Salt Esq. ... to which is added a Detailed Catalogue of Mr. Salt's Collection of Antiquities.* London: John Hearne.

B I–II   A. M. Blackman's notebooks containing a transcription of the text with rough drafts of textual notes and facsimiles. Collated late 1936; pages unnumbered. In School of Archaeology and Oriental Studies, University of Liverpool.

Baines, John 1982, 'Interpreting *Sinuhe*'. *JEA* 68, 31–44.

Barns, John W. B. 1956, *Five Ramesseum Papyri.* Oxford: University Press for Griffith Institute.

Barns MS   Manuscript notes of John W.B. Barns on the Tale in the Griffith Institute (5.10). Undated; pages unnumbered.

Berlev, Oleg Dmitrievich 1966, 'Drevneegipetskaya denezhnaya edinitsa'. *Palestinskii Sbornik* 15, 5–27.

——1987, 'The Date of the "Eloquent Peasant"', in *Form und Mass: Beiträge zur Literatur, Sprache und Kunst des alten Ägypten, Festschrift für Gerhard Fecht*, Jürgen Osing & Günter Dreyer (eds.), 78–83. ÄUAT 12, 1987.

BF   H.W. Fairman's copy of A.M. Blackman's transcription (see 1.1, 1.6), 1936–7(?). (Includes a letter from Gunn). In School of Archaeology and Oriental Studies, University of Liverpool.

Blackman, Aylward M. 1932, *Middle-Egyptian Stories.* BAe 2.

——1934, review of Suys 1933. *JEA* 20, 218–19.

Blumenthal, Elke 1983, 'Ägyptologie und Textkritik'. *OLZ* 78, 229–39.

[Bonomi, Joseph] 1858, *Catalogue of the Egyptian Antiquities in the Museum of Hartwell House.* London: W.M. Watts.

Bosse-Griffiths, Kate 1977, 'A Beset Amulet from the Amarna Period'. *JEA* 63, 98–106.

Bourriau, Janine 1988, *Pharaohs and Mortals: Egyptian Art in the Middle Kingdom*; exhibition catalogue. Cambridge: University Press.

Bruyère, Bernard 1930, *Mert seger à Deir el Médineh*. MIFAO 58.

de Buck, Adriaan 1948, *Egyptian Readingbook* I: *Exercises and Middle Egyptian Texts*. Leiden: Nederlandsch Archaeologisch-Philologisch Instituut voor het Nabije Oosten.

Burkard, Günter 1977, *Textkritische Untersuchungen zu ägyptischen Weisheitslehren des Alten und Mittleren Reiches*. ÄA 34.

Caminos, Ricardo A. 1954, *Late-Egyptian Miscellanies*. Brown Egyptological Studies I. London: Oxford University Press.

——1986 'Some Comments on the Reuse of Papyrus', in *Papyrus: Structure and Usage*, M. L. Bierbrier (ed.), 43–61. British Museum Occasional Paper 60. London: British Museum.

Černý, Jaroslav 1952, *Paper and Books in Ancient Egypt: An Inaugural Lecture Delivered at University College London, 29 May 1947*. London: H. K. Lewis for University College, London.

—— & Alan H. Gardiner, 1957, *Hieratic Ostraca* I. Oxford: University Press for Griffith Institute.

Chabas, François 1863, *Les papyrus hiératiques de Berlin: récits d'il y a quatre mille ans, avec un index géographique et deux planches de fac-simile*. Chalon-sur-Saône: J. Dejussieu. (Reprinted in *Œuvres Diverses* II, 289–364, BÉ 10. Paris: Ernest Leroux 1902).

——1864, 'Sur un texte égyptien relatif au mouvement de la terre'. *ZÄS* 2, 97–103. (Reprinted in *Œuvres Diverses* II, 1–13, BÉ 10. Paris: Ernest Leroux 1902).

David, A. Rosalie 1982, *The Ancient Egyptians: Religious Beliefs and Practices*. London: Routledge & Kegan Paul.

Dawson, Warren R. & Eric P. Uphill 1969, *Who was Who in Egyptology: a Biographical Index of Egyptologists* ... . 2nd edition. London: Oxford University Press for Egypt Exploration Society.

Devauchelle, Didier 1980, 'L'arbre *RDM.T*'. *RdE* 32, 65–8.

Dévaud, Eugène 1911, 'À propos d'un groupe hiératique'. *ZÄS* 49, 106–16.

——1924, *L'Âge des papyrus égyptiens hiératiques d'après les graphies de certains mots: de la XIIe dynastie à la fin de la XVIIIe dynastie*. Paris: Paul Geuthner.

Edel, Elmar 1970, 'Beiträge zum ägyptischen Lexikon V'. *ZÄS* 96, 4–14.

Erman, Adolf 1894, *Ägyptische Grammatik: mit Schrifttafel, Litteratur, Lesestücken und Wörterverzeichnis*. Porta Linguarum Orientalium 15. Berlin: Reuther & Reichard.

——1904, *Aegyptische Chrestomathie: zum Gebrauch auf Universitäten und zum Selbstunterricht*. Porta Linguarum Orientalium 19. Berlin: Reuther & Reichard.

——1923, *Die Literatur der Aegypter: Gedichte, Erzählungen und Lehrbücher aus dem 3. und 2. Jahrtausend v. Chr*. Leipzig: J. C. Hinrichs.

—— & Fritz Krebs 1899, *Aus den Papyrus der Königlichen Museen*. Berlin: W. Spemann.

Faulkner, Raymond O. 1956, 'The Man who was Tired of Life'. *JEA* 42, 21–40.

——1962, *A Concise Dictionary of Middle Egyptian*. Oxford: University Press for Griffith Institute.

——1964, 'Notes on "The Admonitions of an Egyptian Sage"'. *JEA* 50, 24–36.

Fecht, Gerhard 1975, 'Bauerngeschichte'. *LÄ* I, 638–51.

——1982, 'Prosodie'. *LÄ* IV, 1127–54.

Fischer, Henry G. 1968, *Dendera in the Third Millenium B.C.: Down to the Theban Domination of Upper Egypt.* Locust Valley, NY: J. J. Augustin.

Foster, John L. 1984, 'Oriental Institute Ostracon #12074: "Menna's Lament" or "Letter to a Wayward Son"'. *JSSEA* 14, 88–99.

G   Gardiner, Alan H.

Gardiner, Alan H. 1907, 'Eine neue Handschrift des Sinuhegedichtes'. *SPAW* 1907.7, 142–9.

——1909, *Literarische Texte des Mittleren Reiches* II: *Die Erzählung des Sinuhe und die Hirtengeschichte.* Hieratische Papyrus aus den Königlichen Museen zu Berlin 5. Leipzig: J. C. Hinrichs.

——1913, 'Notes on the Story of the Eloquent Peasant'. *PSBA* 35, 264–76.

——1914, 'Notes on the Story of the Eloquent Peasant'. *PSBA* 36, 15–23; 69–74.

——1916, *Notes on the Story of Sinuhe.* Paris: Honoré Champion.

——1923, 'The Eloquent Peasant'. *JEA* 9, 5–25.

——1947, *Ancient Egyptian Onomastica.* 2 vols. text, 1 vol. plates. London: Oxford University Press.

——1955a, *The Ramesseum Papyri.* Oxford: University Press for Griffith Institute.

——1955b, 'A Unique Funerary Liturgy'. *JEA* 41, 9–17.

——1957b, 'Hymns to Sobk in a Ramesseum Papyrus'. *RdE* 11, 43–56, pl. 2–4.

Gilula, Mordechai 1978, 'Peasant B 141–145'. *JEA* 64, 129–30.

Goedicke, Hans 1970a, *The Report about the Dispute of a Man with his* Ba: *Papyrus Berlin 3024.* Baltimore: Johns Hopkins University Press.

——1987, '"Menna's Lament"'. *RdE* 38, 63–80.

Gomaà, Farouk 1987, *Die Besiedlung Ägyptens während des Mittleren Reiches* II: *Unterägypten und die angrenzenden Gebiete.* TAVO Beiheft B 66/2.

Goodwin, Charles W. 1864, 'Lettre à F. Chabas sur un fragment hiératique se rattachant au papyrus de Berlin No. II', in François Chabas, *Mélanges égyptologiques* IIe série, 249–66 [with 'Note du traducteur' (Chabas)]. Chalon-sur-Saône: J. Dejussieu.

Grapow, Hermann 1913, review of Vogelsang 1913. *GGA* 1913:12, 735–51.

Griffith, Francis Ll. 1892, 'Fragments of Old Egyptian Stories from the British Museum and Amherst Collections'. *PSBA* 14, 451–72.

——1898, *The Petrie Papyri: Hieratic Papyri from Kahun and Gurob (principally of the Middle Kingdom).* London: Bernard Quaritch. 2 vols., text and plates.

Guglielmi, Waltraud 1983, 'Eine "Lehre" für einen reiselustigen Sohn'. *WdO* 14, 147–66.

Gunn, Battiscombe G. 1921, 'The Egyptian for "Short"'. *RecTrav* 39, 101–4.

Gunn MS   Two sets of notes by Battiscombe Gunn in the Griffith Institute, Ashmolean Museum, Oxford: Gunn MSS IVA.23 (on the *Eloquent Peasant*); IVB.75 (on P Butler). Undated; pages unnumbered.

Hall, H. R. 1914, 'The Relations of Aegean with Egyptian Art'. *JEA* 1, 197–206.

Hayes, William C. 1955, *A Papyrus of the Late Middle Kingdom in the Brooklyn Museum [Papyrus Brooklyn 35.1446].* Brooklyn: Brooklyn Museum.

Helck, Wolfgang 1974, *Altägyptische Aktenkunde des 3. und 2. Jahrtausends v. Chr.* MÄS 31.

——1981, 'Papyrus Ramesseum E'. *SAK* 9, 151–66.

——1982a, 'Papyri Amherst'. *LÄ* IV, 673–4.

——1982b, 'Papyri Ramesseum'. *LÄ* IV, 726–7.

Hornung, Erik 1978, *Meisterwerke altägyptischer Dichtung.* Zurich & Munich: Artemis.

James, T. G. H. 1962, *The Ḥeḳanakhte Papers and Other Early Middle Kingdom Documents*. PMMA 19.

——*et al.* 1979, *An Introduction to Ancient Egypt*. London: British Museum Publications.

Kemp, Barry J. & Robert S. Merrillees 1980, *Minoan Pottery in Second Millenium Egypt*. SDAIK 12.

Lexa, Franz 1912, 'Beiträge zu der Übersetzung und Erklärung der Geschichte des beredten Bauers'. *RecTrav* 34, 218–31.

Lichtheim, Miriam 1973, *Ancient Egyptian Literature: A Book of Readings* I: *The Old and Middle Kingdoms*. Berkeley: University of California Press.

Luft, Ulrich 1983, 'Illahunstudien, II: ein Verteidigungsbrief aus Illahun'. *Oikumene* 4, 121–79. (Budapest: Akadémiai Kiadó).

M.   citation by sign number of Möller 1927a.

Maas, Paul 1958 [1927], *Textual Criticism* (Barbara Fowler, trans.). Oxford: Clarendon Press.

Maspero, Gaston 1882, *Les contes populaires de l'Égypte ancienne* (Les Littératures populaires de toutes les nations IV). Paris: Maisonneuve.

——1914, review of Vogelsang 1913. *OLZ* 17, 169–74.

Matzker, Ingo 1986, *Die letzen Könige der 12. Dynastie*. Europäische Hochschulschriften, Reihe III: Geschichte und ihre Hilfswissenschaften 297. Frankfurt am Main: Peter Lang.

Megally, Mounir 1971, *Considérations sur les variations et la transformation des formes hiératiques du Papyrus E. 3226 du Louvre*. BdE 49.

——1977, *Notions de comptabilité à propos du Papyrus E. 3226 du Musée du Louvre*. BdE 72.

Miosi, F. T. 1974, 'A Possible Reference to the Non-Calendar Week'. *ZÄS* 101, 150–52.

Möller, Georg 1927a, *Hieratische Paläographie: die ägyptische Buchschrift in ihrer Entwicklung von der fünften Dynastie bis zur römischen Kaiserzeit* I: *Bis zum Beginn der achtzehnten Dynastie*. 2nd edition. Leipzig: J. C. Hinrichs.

——1927b, *Hieratische Lesestücke für den akademischen Gebrauch* I: *Alt- und mittelhieratische Texte*. Leipzig: J. C. Hinrichs.

——1936, *Hieratische Paläographie: die ägyptische Buchschrift in ihrer Entwicklung von der fünften Dynastie bis zur römischen Kaiserzeit: Erzänzungsheft zu Band I und II*. Leipzig: J. C. Hinrichs.

Morenz, Siegfried 1975 [1969], 'Die Bedeutungsentwicklung von 𓈖𓂝𓈖𓅂 *"Das, was kommt" zu "Unheil" und "Unrecht"*', in *id., Religion und Geschichte des alten Ägypten: gesammelte Aufsätze*, Elke Blumenthal *et al.* (eds.), 343–60. Weimar: Hermann Böhlaus Nachfolger.

Müller, W. Max 1893, 'The Story of the Peasant'. *PSBA* 15, 343–4.

Newberry, Percy M. 1899, *The Amherst Papyri: Being an Account of the Egyptian Papyri in the Collection of the Right Hon. Lord Amherst of Hackney* . . . . London: Bernard Quaritch.

P   Perry 1986.

Parkinson, R. B. 1988, *The Tale of the Eloquent Peasant: A Commentary*. Doctoral thesis: Oxford University.

Perry, Evelyn 1986, *A Critical Study of the* Eloquent Peasant. Dissertation: Johns Hopkins University. Ann Arbor: University Microfilms.

Petrie, W. M. Flinders 1895, *Egyptian Tales translated from the Papyri: First series, IVth to XIIth dynasty*. London: Methuen.

Plas, Dirk van der 1986, *L'Hymne à la crue du Nil*. 2 vols. Egyptologische Uitgaven 4. Leiden: Nederlands Instituut voor het Nabije Oosten.

Posener, Georges 1951a, 'Les richesses inconnues de la littérature égyptienne (Recherches littéraires I)'. *RdE* 6, 27–48.

——1951b, 'Sur l'emploi de l'encre rouge dans les manuscrits égyptiens'. *JEA* 37, 75–80.

——1955, '*Urk.* IV, 139, 2–7'. *RdE* 10, 92–4.

——1956, *Littérature et politique dans l'Égypte de la XIIe dynastie*. BEHE 307.

——1969, 'Fragment littéraire de Moscou'. *MDAIK* 25, 101–6.

Quibell, J. E. 1898, *The Ramesseum*. ERA 2, 1–21, pl. 1–30a.

S   Suys 1933.

Schäfer, Heinrich, 1902–3, 'Eine kursive Form von 𓆳'. *ZÄS* 40, 121–4.

Schenkel, Wolfgang 1978, *Das Stemma der altägyptischen Sonnenlitanei: Grundlegung der Textgeschichte nach der Methode der Textkritik*. GOF IV.6.

Sethe, Kurt 1927, *Erläuterungen zu den ägyptischen Lesestücken: Texte des Mittleren Reiches*. Leipzig: J. C. Hinrichs.

——1928a, *Aegyptische Lesestücke zum Gebrauch im akademischen Unterricht: Texte des Mittleren Reiches*. 2nd edition. Leipzig: J. C. Hinrichs.

——1928b, *Dramatische Texte zu altägyptischen Mysterienspielen*. UGAÄ 10.

Simpson, William Kelly 1958, 'Allusions to *The Shipwrecked Sailor* and *The Eloquent Peasant* in a Ramesside Text'. *JAOS* 78, 50–51.

——1963, *Papyrus Reisner I: The Records of a Building Project in the Reign of Sesostris I, Transcription and Commentary*. Boston: Museum of Fine Arts.

——1972, 'Papyri of the Middle Kingdom', in *Textes et langages de l'Egypte pharaonique*, Serge Sauneron (ed.), II, 63–72. BdE 64/2.

——1984, 'Sinuhe'. *LÄ* V, 950–55.

Smither, Paul 1939, 'A New Reading of *Lebensmüde*, 131–2'. *JEA* 25, 220.

——1945, 'The Semnah Despatches'. *JEA* 31, 3–10.

Spalinger, Anthony J. 1984, 'Sobekhotep II'. *LÄ* V, 1037–9.

Spanel, Donald B. 1984, 'Semna Papyri'. *LÄ* V, 844–7.

Sturtewagen, Christian *et al.* 1985, 'A Few Additions to O. Chicago 12074'. *Discussions in Egyptology* 1, 47–9.

Suys, Émile 1933, *Étude sur le conte du fellah plaideur: récit égyptien du Moyen-Empire*. AnOr 5. Rome: Pontificio Istituto Biblico.

Tait, W. J. 1986, 'Guidelines and Borders in Demotic Papyri', in *Papyrus: Structure and Usage*, M. L. Bierbrier (ed.), 63–89. British Museum Occasional Paper 60. London: British Museum.

Tigay, Jeffrey H. 1985, 'Introduction', in *Empirical Models for Biblical Criticism*, Jeffrey Tigay (ed.), 1–20. Philadelphia: University of Pennsylvania Press.

Turner, Eric G. 1978, 'The Terms Recto and Verso: the Anatomy of the Papyrus Roll', in *Actes du XVe Congrès International de Papyrologie* 1, 1–71. Papyrologica Bruxellensia 16. Brussels: Fondation Égyptologique Reine Élisabeth.

V   Vogelsang 1913.

Vernus, Pascal 1990, 'La date du *Paysan Eloquent*', in *Studies in Egyptology Presented to Miriam Lichtheim*, Sarah Israelit-Groll (ed.), 1033–47. Jerusalem: Magnes Press for Publications of the Department of Egyptology in the Hebrew University of Jerusalem.

VG   Vogelsang & Gardiner 1908.

Vogelsang, Friedrich 1904, *Die Klagen des Bauern (aus Papyrus 3023 und 3025 der Königlichen Museen zu Berlin)*. Inaugural- Dissertation: Friedrich-Wilhelms-Universität zu Berlin. Berlin: Bernhard Paul.

——1913, *Kommentar zu den Klagen des Bauern*. UGAÄ 6.

—— & Alan H. Gardiner 1908, *Literarische Texte des Mittleren Reiches* IV: *Die Klagen des Bauern*. Hieratische Papyrus aus den Königlichen Museen zu Berlin 4. Leipzig: J. C. Hinrichs.

Wente, Edward F. 1965, 'A Note on "The Eloquent Peasant" BI 13–15'. *JNES* 24, 105–9.

Westendorf, Wolfhart 1977, 'Das strandende Schiff: zur Lesung und Übersetzung von Bauer BI, 58 = R 101', in *Fragen an die altägyptische Literatur: Studien zum Gedenken an Eberhard Otto*, Jan Assmann et al. (eds.), 503–9. Wiesbaden: Dr. Ludwig Reichert.

Yoyotte, Jean 1957, review of Gardiner 1955a. *RdE* 11, 172–5.

CONCORDANCES
OF LINE NUMBERS

B1

Old	New	Old	New	Old	New
A.A 1	1–14	18	49	54	85
2	15	19	50	55	86
3	16	20	51	56	87
4	17	21	52	57	88
5	18	22	53	58	89
6	19	23	54	59	90
A.B 7	20	24	55	60	91
8	21	25	56	61	92
9	22	26	57	62	93
10	23	27	58	63	94
A.C 11	24	28	59	64	95
12	25	29	60	65	96
13	26	30	61	66	97
14	27	31	62	67	98
15	28	32	63	68	99
A.D–E		33	64	69	100
16	29	34	65	70	101
17	30	35	66	71	102
18	31	36	67	72	103
B1 1	32	37	68	73	104
2	33	38	69	74	105
3	34	39	70	75	106
4	35	40	71	76	107
5	36	41	72	77	108
6	37	42	73	78	109
7	38	43	74	79	110
8	39	44	75	80	111
9	40	45	76	81	112
10	41	46	77	82	113
11	42	47	78	83	114
12	43	48	79	84	115
13	44	49	80	85	116
14	45	50	81	86	117
15	46	51	82	87	118
16	47	52	83	88	119
17	48	53	84	89	120

Old	New	Old	New	Old	New
90	121	134	165	178	209
91	122	135	166	179	210
92	123	136	167	180	211
93	124	137	168	181	212
94	125	138	169	182	213
95	126	139	170	183	214
96	127	140	171	184	215
97	128	141	172	185	216
98	129	142	173	186	217
99	130	143	174	187	218
100	131	144	175	188	219
101	132	145	176	189	220
102	133	146	177	190	221
103	134	147	178	191	222
104	135	148	179	192	223
105	136	149	180	193	224
106	137	150	181	194	225
107	138	151	182	195	226
108	139	152	183	196	227
109	140	153	184	197	228
110	141	154	185	198	229
111	142	155	186	199	230
112	143	156	187	200	231
113	144	157	188	201	232
114	145	158	189	202	233
115	146	159	190	203	234
116	147	160	191	204	235
117	148	161	192	205	236
118	149	162	193	206	237
119	150	163	194	207	238
120	151	164	195	208	239
121	152	165	196	209	240
122	153	166	197	210	241
123	154	167	198	211	242
124	155	168	199	212	243
125	156	169	200	213	244
126	157	170	201	214	245
127	158	171	202	215	246
128	159	172	203	216	247
129	160	173	204	217	248
130	161	174	205	218	249
131	162	175	206	219	250
132	163	176	207	220	251
133	164	177	208	221	252

Old	New	Old	New	Old	New
222	253	257	288	293	324
223	254	258	289	294	325
224	255	259	290	295	326
225	256	260	291	296	327
226	257	261	292	297	328
227	258	262	293	298	329
228	259	263	294	299	330
229	260	264	295	300	331
230	261	265	296	301	332
231	262	266	297	302	333
232	263	267	298	303	334
233	264	268	299	304	335
234	265	269	300	305	336
235	266	270	301	306	337
236	267	271	302	307	338
237	268	272	303	308	339
238	269	273	304	309	340
239	270	274	305	310	341
240	271	275	306	311	342
241	272	276	307	312	343
242	273	277	308	313	344
243	274	278	309	314	345
244	275	279	310	315	346
245	276	280	311	316	347
246	277	281	312	317	348
247	278	282	313	318	349
248	279	283	314	319	350
249	280	284	315	320	351
250	281	285	316	321	352
251	282	286	317	322	353
252	283	287	318	323	354
253	284	288	319	324	355
254	285	289	320	325	356
255	286	290	321	326	357
256	287	291	322		
		292	323		

R

(v) marks a line as vertical; this is numbered as the last line of the preceding column of horizontal lines.

Old	New	Old	New	Old	New
1	1.1	40	6.6	79	12.2
2	1.2	41	6.7	80	12.3
3	1.3	42	7.1	81	12.4
4	1.4	43	7.2	82	12.5
5	1.5	44	7.3	83	12.6
6	1.6	45	7.4	84	12.7
7	1.7	46	7.5	85	12.8
8	2.1	47	7.6	86	13.1
9	2.2	48	7.7	87	13.2
10	2.3	49	8.1	88	13.3
11	2.4	50	8.2	89	13.4
12	2.5	51	8.3	90	13.5
13	2.6	52	8.4	91	13.6
14	2.7	53	8.5	92	13.7
15	3.1	54	8.6	93	13.8
16	3.2	55	8.7	94	13.9(v)
17	3.3	56	8.8(v)	95	13.10(v)
18	3.4	57	9.1	96	14.1
19	3.5	58	9.2	97	14.2
20	3.6	59	9.3	98	14.3
21	3.7	60	9.4	99	14.4
22	4.1	61	9.5	100	14.5
23	4.2	62	9.6	101	14.6
24	4.3	63	9.7	102	14.7
25	4.4	64	10.1	103	15.1
26	4.5	65	10.2	104	15.2
27	4.6	66	10.3	104	15.3
28	4.7	67	10.4	106	15.4
29	5.1	68	10.5	107	15.5
30	5.2	69	10.6	108	15.6
31	5.3	70	10.7	109	15.7
32	5.4	71	11.1	110	16.1
33	5.5	72	11.2	111	16.2
34	5.6	73	11.3	112	16.3
35	6.1	74	11.4	113	16.4
36	6.2	75	11.5	114	16.5
37	6.3	76	11.6	115	16.6
38	6.4	77	11.7	116	16.7
39	6.5	78	12.1	117	16.8

Old	New		Old	New		Old	New
118	17.1					186	26.5
119	17.2		Lacuna			187	26.6
120	17.3					188	26.7
121	17.4		160	23.4		189	26.8
122	17.5		161	23.5		190	27.1
123	17.6		162	23.6		191	27.2
124	17.7		163	23.7		192	27.3
125	18.1		164	24.1		193	27.4
126	18.2		165	24.2		194	27.5
127	18.3		166	24.3		195	27.6
128	18.4		167	24.4		196	27.7
129	18.5		168	24.5		197	27.8
130	18.6		169	24.6			
131	18.7		170	24.7		Lacuna	
132	19.1		171	25.1			
133	19.2		172	25.2		219	30.6
134	19.3		173	25.3		220	30.7
135	19.4		174	25.4		{221}★	
136	19.5		175	25.5		222	31.1
137	19.6		176	25.3		223	31.2
138	19.7		177	25.4		224	31.3
139	20.1		178	25.5		225	31.4
140	20.2		179	25.6		226	31.5
141	20.3		180	25.7		227	31.6
142	20.4		181	25.8		228	31.7
143	20.5		182	26.1		229	31.8
144	20.6		183	26.2			
145	20.7		184	26.3		★This line, restored by	
146	21.1		185	26.4		VG, did not exist.	

THE TALE OF
THE ELOQUENT PEASANT

CONVENTIONS

The full forms of ![glyph], ![glyph] and ![glyph] are not distinguished from the abbreviated forms, as is standard practice; see 1.3.

Ligatures are not commented on unless the reading is uncertain.

¹⁴| a line break, with the number of the following line above

> A blank space shows that the passage is not found in this manuscript. In B2 82 the manuscript contains an actual blank space, which is recorded in the notes.

![glyph]   written in red ink

?   an illegible sign

![glyph]   an uncertain, but probable, reading

![glyph]   a damaged area

![glyph]   an extensive damaged area, with an indication of the estimated number of sign groups lost

> Restorations are marked as hatched signs, and are given wherever legible traces are preserved; the preserved areas of the signs are left unhatched. If the trace is too slight to indicate thus, it is marked 'tr.'. Apart from the completion of half-preserved word groups, no restoration is made without a supporting parallel. Where there is the possibility of a textual or orthographic variant against the preserved parallel of another manuscript, there is again no restoration, unless such a variant is found consistently elsewhere. Restorations are made within the text only where the arrangement of signs is reasonably certain; other restorations are given in the notes.

Facsimiles are provided when the reading is uncertain or has been disputed; the facsimiles of groups are approximately 1 : 1. They have been collated with the photographs in VG and the copies in *LD*, which often preserve traces now lost; collations are noted only where these sources are significant. Traces of ink are indicated by hatching.

Past readings are given wherever it is judged appropriate. Contrary opinions to, and arguments against, many readings of Suys are not listed, as his errors are apparent from the facsimiles.

THE TALE OF
THE ELOQUENT PEASANT

2.a Clear traces:

4.a So G 1923:22. Contra VG pl.1a ( ). Cf. R 1.6.

5.a Clear traces: Contra S:2–3* ( ); G 1923:7 ('last harvest'); Lichtheim 1973:171 ('last year'); Hornung 1978:9 ('Ernte').

5.b Traces: Cf. M.619 (Illahun). So BF:48. Contra S:2* ( ), for which there is insufficient room.

6.a Traces: Surface damaged. 'Traces suit neither *wn* nor *sp*' (G 1923:22). Perhaps restore ; contra S:2–3* ( ).

7.a Contra S:2* (. His ⌐ is the end of the *'q*-bird, distorted by break; cf. R 11.4).

8.a Traces: So Sethe 1928a:18.2 n.a, BF:49. Contra V:29 (*'nḫ:j*); G 1923:7 ('travel': *šm=j*).

9.a In all mss the following list is arranged in vertical columns, with the determinatives in a subcolumn (VG pl.1; Griffith 1892 pl.1; fig.1). This format is retained here.

?	B1
	Bt
	R

?	B1
	Bt
	R

?	B1
	Bt
	R

?	B1
	Bt
	R

5

10

2.a/3.a   🦅 set to right of main column.

5.a   See 6.a

6.a   So VG pl.1a. Contra G 1923:22 ( ). See
       Dévauchelle 1980.

8.a   The scribe started to write ⁞⁞, then changed
       to ⁞⁞.

11.a   Apparently more like 𝄃𝄃 than ⌒ , but tick
        above ⌒ is part of ∫ .

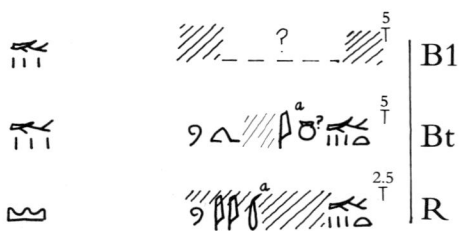

		B1
		Bt
		R

		B1
		Bt
		R

5

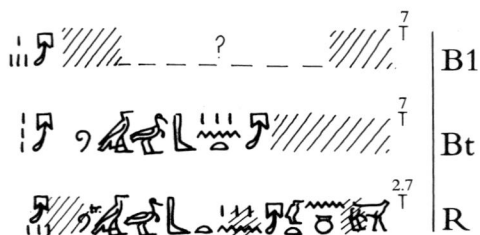

		B1
		Bt
		R

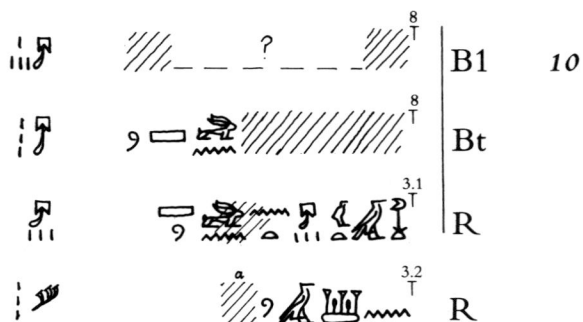

		B1
		Bt
		R
		R

10

2.a Traces:  The restorations of Edel 1970:7
(Bt: ⲟ ⲁ[ⲟⲟⲟ], R: ⲟⲟⲟⲟ[ⲟⲟ]) are
impossible (contra Gomaà 1987:286–7).

3.a Traces: ⲟⲟⲟⲟ See 2.a

13.a Faint traces: ⲟ ⲟ ⲟⲟ was written in the wrong place,
then erased and rewritten.

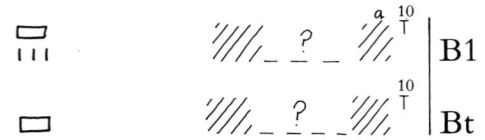

5

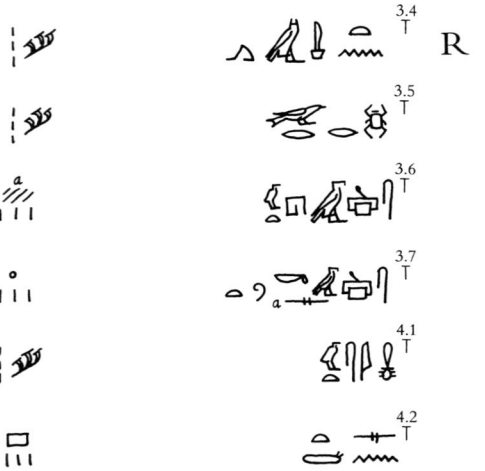

10

1.a/4.a   Identification of B1 and Bt 9–10 with items in the list of R is uncertain. Determinatives suggest that they correspond to R 3.3 (*'nw*) and 4.2 (*snt*), or 4.3 (*'b*[*3*]). Length of lacunae in B1 and Bt suit either alternative.

8.a   Traces: Perhaps .

9.a   ─ᴴ─ placed below line in darker ink: a later addition.

R

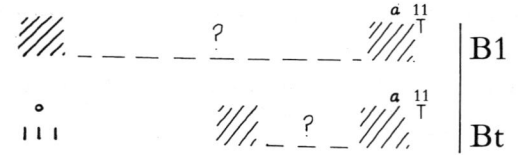

B1

Bt

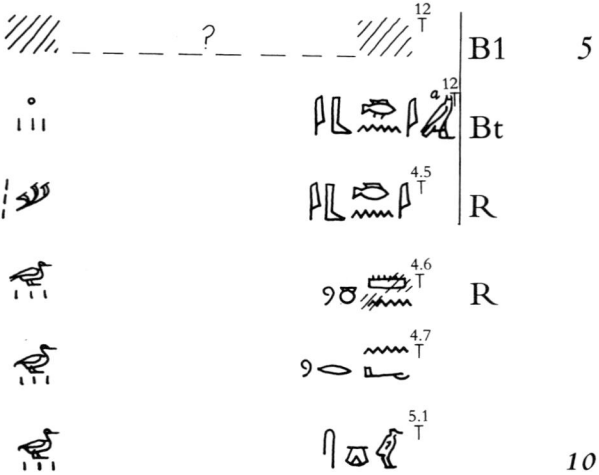

B1   5

Bt

R

R

10

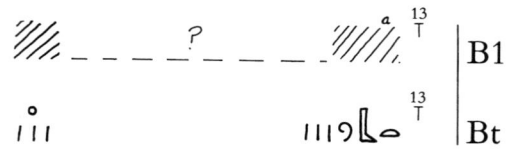

B1

Bt

1.a Traces, which suit the reading  : 

3.a/4.a It is uncertain to which item in R these lacunae correspond. Although the determinative in Bt suggests *s3hwt* (R 3.6) or *s3kswt* (R 3.7), *jbs3* (R 4.4) is also possible (cf. determinatives for *jnbj* in Bt 12 and R 4.5).

6.a See 2a.2.a. Second column of the list of goods begins here.

11.a See 2a.2.a. Second column of the list of goods begins here. This item may correspond with *tbsw* in R 5.3 – perhaps read *tb<s>w*.

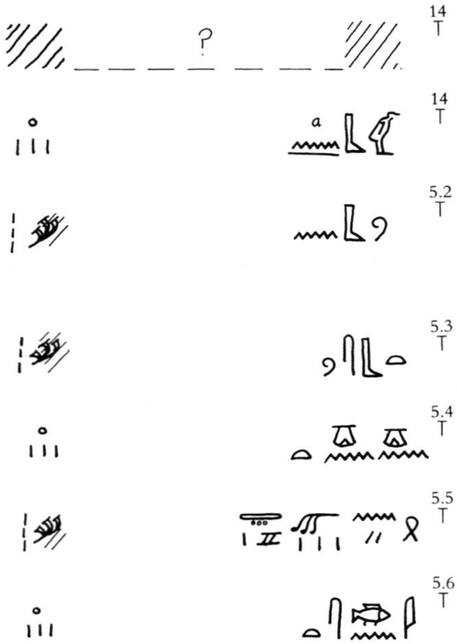

B1
Bt
R

R

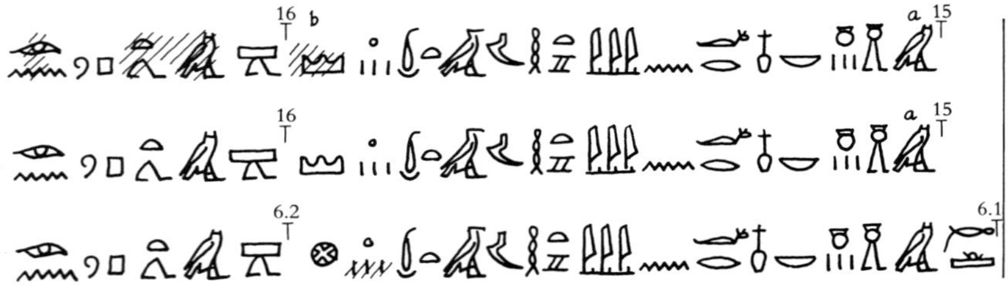

B1
Bt
R

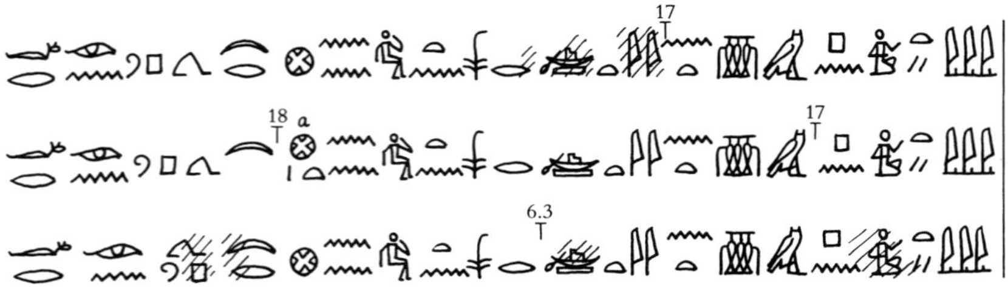

B1
Bt
R

2.a   Added in red, a later correction over erased signs; the remains of one of these
       forms the stroke-like trace over Bt 15 (see pp. xxi–xxii).

8.a   B1 15–6 short, placed under final item of the second column of
       the list of goods.

8.b   This shorter than B1 16, unless additonal sign lost: unlikely.

9.a   As in B1 (8.a). Writing cramped; Bt 15–6 longer at bottom than
       following lines, to accomodate same number of signs.

12.a   Now no trace of the spacefiller/blot under group shown in
       Griffith 1892 pl.1.

	B1
	Bt
	R

	B1	
	Bt	5
	R	

	B1
	Bt
	R

	B1	10
	Bt	
	R	

1.a ⬅

4.a In B1 ⌒❘⚡ is very similar to cursive ⨎ . For this reading, see
Berlev 1969; contra Schäfer 1902–3, VG pl.1a *et al.* (⸗🐎).
Previous readings: Chabas 1863:6; Goodwin 1864:255; Griffith
1892:463, 466 (⌒⸗✚); Müller 1893, Newberry 1899:17 (⸗👤⌒).

5.a Reading certain; Gunn read ⚥ without ❘ (MS), but cf. Bt 18, 36.

5.b. Apparently corrected out of a ⌣ .

8.a Written to left of line due to lack of space; added later.

B1

Bt

R

B1

Bt

R

B1

Bt

R

B1

Bt

R

5

10

5.a Cramped at bottom of long line.

10.a   See Dévaud 1911; Blackman 1932:47a.2a; James 1962:94.

12.a   *w't* is cramped to avoid long line. ǀ was once clearly visible (VG pl.1a).

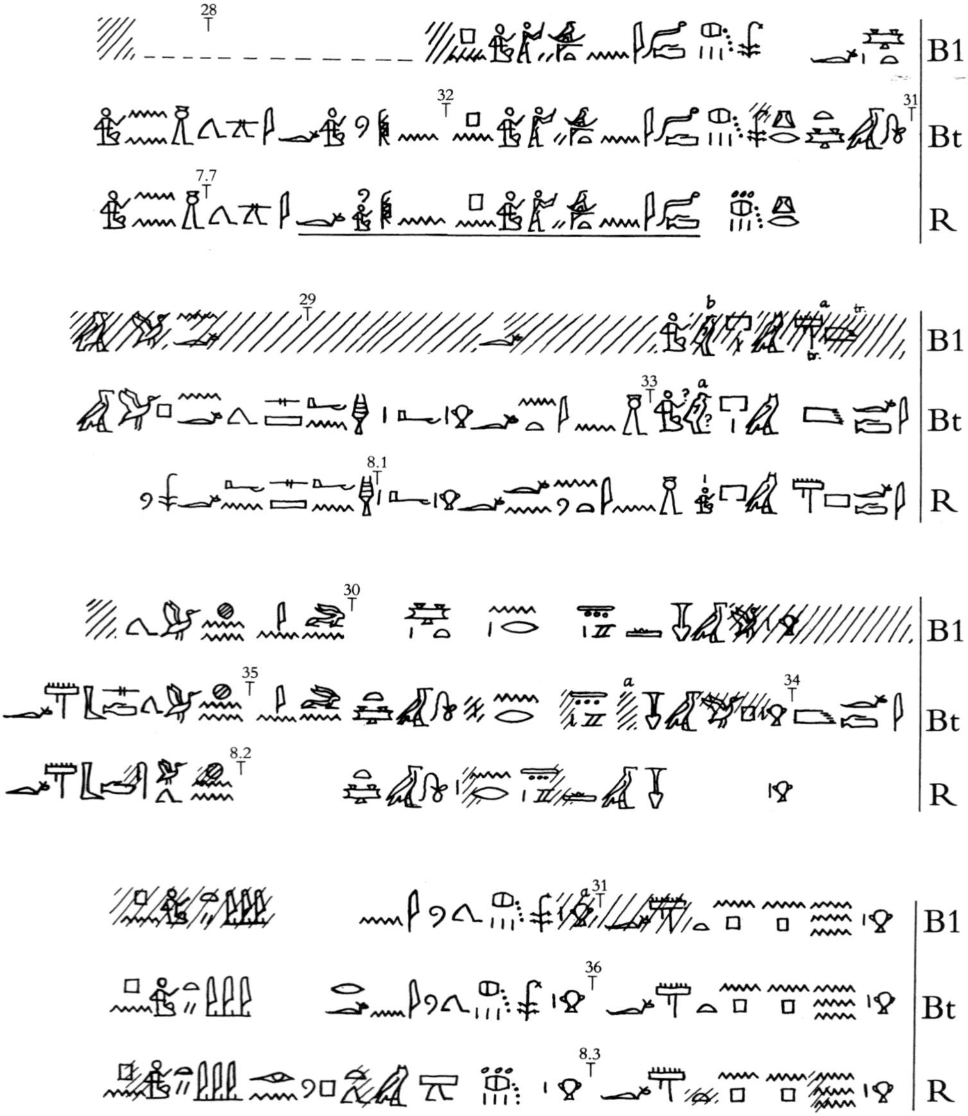
B1
Bt
R
B1
Bt
R
B1
Bt
R
B1
Bt
R

4.a So BF:53; contra Möller 1927b:13(𓄿 ⬭).

4.b Clear traces: So Möller 1927b:13. Contra
                                   Grifffith 1892:464, Newberry
                                   1899:17 (//𓎯). Final sign unlike
                                   // .

5.a   So Möller 1927b:13. Contra
                                   Griffith 1892:464 (𓄿 ⬭); V:39,
                                   Sethe 1928a:19, S:5*, BF:53 (𓏠).
                                   The reading 𓀐 + a space-
                                   filler (cf. Bt 17; 6a.12.a) is
                                   also possible; see 4.b.

8.a Probably no loss.

10.a Exact placing of line division uncertain (so Möller 1927a:13–4).

B1

Bt

R

B1

Bt

R

B1

Bt

R

B1

R

2.a   Written to one side due to lack of space.

6.a   Too large for ⌓ ?

11.a   R 8.8 is a vertical line, spaciously written, allowing column 9 to start with a rubric.

B1

R

B1

R

B1 5

R

B1

R

B1

R

B1 10

R

B1

R

1.a So Möller 1936:4 (Sinuhe 194); see also Smither 1939.

3.a So BF:54, G 1923:22. Large like ⬭.

5.a Written to one side, making B1 40 a short line.

6.a Traces: The restoration ~~~~ is impossible (VG pl.2a), and ~~~~ practically certain.

B1		
R		

B1
R

B1   5
R

B1
R

B1
R   10

B1
R

1.a   So Berlev 1966:8–9. Contra Wente 1965:105 *et al.* (⌐|).

1.b   So Berlev 1966:8, 13, *passim*. Contra V:49, VG pl.5a (⌂); S:6* (◯ ⌂); Wente 1965:106–7; for other earlier readings see Wente 1965:105.
The ⌐ is written to one side.

1.c   Contra VG pl.5a, reading ⌐ due to a tick.

2.a   See 1.a

2.b   So Berlev 1966:8, 13, *passim*. Contra V:49, VG pl.2a, S:7* (? ⌐); BF:55 (▽); Wente 1965:107 (⌐ ; doubtful about ⌒). ⌒ may derive from the related *šnꜥ* (Wb. IV,504.5–505.13: Berlev 1966:23).

2.c   See Wente 1965:107 n.34. Contra S:7* (⌐|◯); Berlev 1966:8 (blot).

6.a   Not ⊢⊣ ; cf. M.325.

8.a   So BF:55. No trace of any following sign (i.e. ▽).

8.b   Traces:

B1

R

B1

R

B1

R

5

B1

R

B1

R

B1

R

10

B1

R

11.a   Full writing, distinct from .

11.b   Cramped at bottom of long line.

12.a   Obscured by fibres from another sheet, inseparable in unrolling.

B1

R

B1

R

B1   5

R

B1

R

B1

R   10

B1

R

1.a Ligature, with large ⌒ .

2.a Room to restore 𓀔 as in 11.7.

3.a 𓏤 So G 1923:22, BF:57, Miosi 1974:151. Contra VG pl.6a (☰); M.659; B1 uses numbers with both horizontal and vertical strokes, but this is clearly not ⊃ as in B1 225.

4.a–b Traces: 𓂝𓏏𓏭𓄿

5.a 𓏤 See 3.a.

6.a 𓊪 Erroneous stroke distinct from 𓏲 of the line above (R 12.3). Perhaps read 〰〰 , or as dittography of 𓈖𓂋 ?

[hieroglyphic text, line 68]	B1
[hieroglyphic text]	R
[hieroglyphic text, lines 70, 69, 13.2]	B1
[hieroglyphic text]	R
[hieroglyphic text, line 71]	B1
[hieroglyphic text, line 13.3]	R
[hieroglyphic text, lines 73, 72]	B1
[hieroglyphic text, line 13.4]	R
[hieroglyphic text, line 74]	B1
[hieroglyphic text, line 13.5]	R
[hieroglyphic text, line 75]	B1
[hieroglyphic text, line 13.6]	R

5

10

4.a Traces: ![glyph]

4.b For restoration cf. R 13.3.

8.a ⌒⌣ at end of R 13.3 is faint (though not purposely deleted). The size of the lacuna at start of R 13.4 suggests a dittography of ⌒⌣ is to be restored there.

9.a The orthography of *srw* with ![glyph], often formed as if ![glyph], is peculiar to the scribe of B1 and P Berlin 3022 (*Sinuhe*: B 184); see Dévaud 1924: no.13. It arises from the similarity of ![glyph] and ![glyph] in hieratic (cf. B1 163, 327, 328, 332).

B1
R

B1
R

B1   5
R

B1
R

B1   10
R

B1
R

2.a ⟨glyph⟩ So Gunn (BF), BF:58. Contra VG pl.3a *et al*. (⟨glyphs⟩).

4.a Traces: ⟨glyph⟩ suit □ but not ⌢. Restore ⟨glyph⟩, rather than ⟨glyph⟩ (BF:58).

8.a Restore ⟨glyphs⟩, for which just enough room.

	B1
	R
	B1
	R
	B1
	R
	B1
	R
	B1
	R
	B1
	R

5

10

4.a   Traces: Contra BF:59 ( ); restoration suits space.

7.a   See G 1923:22.

8.a   No trace of ⌒ above 𝕮 ; restoration suits space.

9.a   Contra S:9*, who read thus but commented: 'pour ⌀ ⫯ 𝄄 '. See 10.a.

10.a   See Westendorf 1977:505–6. Contra VG pl.3a (▨▨▨ 𝄄 ⟆); V:65 (⟆ 𝄄 ⟆ ⟆?); S:9*, BF:60 (⟆ ⟆).

12.a Short line.

12.b So VG pl.3a, Posener 1955:93 n.2. Contra V:65, G 1916:99 (⟆).

12.c Traces:

	B1
	R

5

10

1.a   Omission of ⌴ perhaps due to lack of space at line end.

3.a   So Grapow 1913:743, G 1923:22; contra VG pl.7a (⚹ ?).

4.a/6.a   Traces: ∪   (fibres realigned). Restoration
                                          uncertain: ... or ...（B I,57)?

5.a   ⌒ to one side.

6.b   So B I,57.

10.a   Traces:

11.a   Added later.

[Hieroglyphic text for B1 (lines 101, 100)] | B1

[Hieroglyphic text for R (lines 16.5, 16.4)] | R

[Hieroglyphic text for B1] | B1

[Hieroglyphic text for R (lines 16.7, 16.6)] | R

4.a Just space to restore ⌗⌗ (so BF:61; contra S:28 [_ḥr_]).

6.a Very faint.

6.b Traces: ⌗⌗ ⌗⌗ . Contra B 1,61 (⌗⌗).

7.a Written as a single horizontal group, wider than the line.

8.a Obscured by sign from unrelated fibres inseparable in unrolling.

a 108	B1
	R
109	B1
17.6	R
111 ... 110	B1
17.7	R
	B1
18.1 *a*	R
a 112	B1
18.2	R
113	B1
c 18.4 ... *b* ... *c*.3 ... 18.3 *a*	R

5

10

1.a   Short vertical line, inset into a column of horizontal lines. B1 109–45 is written in columns of horizontal lines.

4.a   Traces:

8.a   Traces:

8.b   Traces of a stroke under ⚱.

9.a   Contra VG pl.7a ( ) 'sehr kursiv'; for *'nḫt* see Faulkner 1964:31). Cf. B1 113; VG's ⌒ may be merely a tick at the end of the ligature, or to be read ⌇⌇⌇ (cf. M.xviii n.1).

10.a   Traces: Cf. R 18.7; space to restore .

12.a   Traces:

12.b   Uncertain traces: Contra VG pl.4a ( ); VG pl.4 bis a ( ); S:11* ( ).

12.c   Traces:

114   B1

18.5   *a* 4-5   R

115   B1

18.6   R

18.7   R   5

116   B1

117   B1

     B1

19.2   19.1   R

118   B1   10

19.3   R

     B1

19.5   19.4   R

2.a Traces: 2.b Traces:

3.a   apparently with extra stroke, as if ⌣ . As in B1 118.

3.b The two ⌣ s are run together into a single stroke. Contra VG pl.7a (⌣).

5.a Traces: Restore ⎯ , followed by ⌣ with a long line (so S:11*).

6.a   See 14a.3.a. So G 1923:22–3, BF:64, which is supported by the context. Contra VG pl.7a, S:10* (‖‖‖).

7.a   So BF:63. Contra S:10*.

10.a   See 3.a

10.b   So BF:63 (cf. Blackman 1934:218, reading ‖‖ ⌣); for this orthography see Fischer 1968:94. Contra VG pl.7a ( ); G 1923:23 ( ); Sethe 1928a:23.14–5 ( ); S:10* ( ).

11.a   Contra VG pl.4 bis a, Blackman 1934:218 (·); S:11* ( ). Cf. M.695, 709, James 1962: Pal.15.

13.a   For restoration cf. R 19.2.

R

B1

R

B1

R

5

B1

R

B1

R

B1

R

10

B1

R

B1

R

1.a Restore ⳦ with numeral, perhaps '10' (for the ratio of bread to beer see *Siût* I.314, P Westcar 7.1–2).

1.b Contra G 1923:22 (⳦).

3.a Restoration necessary unless line short (cf. R 19.7).

3.b Short line (unless ⳦ is to be restored: unlikely).

3.c The exact restoration is uncertain. Number of groups lost uncertain – all but a full line.

5.a To judge by other rubrics and following traces, this lacuna is longer than as now mounted and as shown in VG pl.4 bis. Fragment I should be some 2 cm further left; R 20.5, 20.6 were probably shorter lines than R 20.1.

5.b Illegible traces:

VG pl.4 bis a suggests ⳦ , which is just possible. ⳦ is presumably to be restored between end of traces copied here and ⳦ .

9.a Traces: Perhaps read ⳦ .

10.a B1 121 is a half line, ending column.

11.a Traces: Restore ⳦ .

13.a Unidentifiable traces at end of 20.7: Perhaps ⳦ of *nwdw* (= B1 123)?

B1

5

10

1.a   [glyph]   So VG pl.8a, BF:64. Contra S:10* ([glyph]).

5.a   [glyph]   So G 1923:23, BF:64, S:11* (cf. P Edwin Smith 2.1). Contra VG pl.8a ([glyph]). Cf. 28a.9.b.

5.b Large but certain.   5.c   See M.145; G 1923:23; cf. 29a.5.a.

6.a   [glyph]   So G 1923:23 (for *wtḥ*); BF:64. Contra VG pl.8a ([glyph] ; cf. Grapow 1913:744–5); S:10* ([glyph]).

7.a   [glyph]   Contra G 1923:23, BF:64 ([glyph]); S:10* ([glyph]). Elsewhere in B1 *jt* is invariably determined with [glyph].

7.b   [glyph]   So VG pl.8a *et al.*

8.a   [glyph]   Contra S:12* ([glyph] ; see S:48).

8.b   [glyph]   So G 1923:23, BF:64. Contra VG pl.8a ([glyph]).

9.a   [glyph]   Contra S:12* ([glyph] ; see S:48).

10.a   [glyph]   [glyph]   So G 1923:23. Contra VG pl.8a ([glyph] + [glyph]); S:12* ([glyph] + [glyph]).

10.b   [glyph]   So G 1923:23, BF:64. Contra VG pl.8a, S:12* ([glyph]).

10.c   [glyph]   So G 1923:23 'probably no importance is to be attached to the unusual form'. Contra VG pl.8a ([glyph]); S:12* ([glyph] ; see Blackman 1934:218).

11.a [glyph] first written at level of top of [glyph] and then obliterated.

138

B1

139 a

141
b

140

142

5

143
b

c

144

146
c

145
b

a

147

a

148

150

149

10

151
a

B1

R

23.1

152
a

B1

b 23.3

23.2
a

R

2.a   So BF:65; see G 1923:23, 11 n.8. Contra VG pl.8a ( ); S:12* (?).

2.b   Contra VG pl.8a *et al.* (∼∼∼); cf. ◁ in B1 209. Cursive, but certain.

2.c   So Gunn 1921:102, G 1923:23, BF:65 (for ḥw'). Contra V:97 ( ); S:12* ( ).

3.a   Faint ◠ under ◁ intentionally erased.

3.b   Contra S:12* (=).   4.a   So BF:65; very like a ⌒ .

5.a   So BF:65. Contra VG pl.8a *et al.* ( ).

5.b   corrected over a faint , intentionally erased.

5.c   So G 1923:23. Contra VG pl.8a, S:12* ( ).

7.a   So VG pl.8a *et al.*   7.b   Short line ending column. B1 146–52 are vertical lines.

7.c   So VG pl.9a, G 1923:23, noting 'the supposed *r* more like ⌐ *d*'. Contra BF:65 ( ); S:12–3* (; his division of ◠ and ∼∼∼ is due to damaged fibres).

8.a   Contra VG pl.9a ( ); G 1923:23, BF:65 ( ); S:12–3* ( ).

11.a   So G 1923:23. Contra VG pl.9a, S:12* ( ).

13.a   So BF:65, G 1923:23. Contra VG pl.9a, S:12* ( ).

14.a   Traces of ⏐ were once visible, but lost by 1936 (B I,83).

14.b   Traces: The top trace is ⌒ , from the end of R 22.3. Read perhaps (=B1 147).

B1

R

B1

R

B1

R

5

B1

R

B1

R

B1

R

10

B1

R

1.a   Traces: So Dévaud (Grapow 1913:745–6), doubted by G 1923:23; cf. B1 156. Contra VG pl.9a ( ); S:12* ( ).

1.b   B1 153–217 written in columns of horizontal lines.

2.a   Traces: ⁓ may be ⌇⌇⌇.

2.b   Traces: For full form of ⫰ in R cf. R 5.1, R 13.10.

2.c   Traces:

3.a   Palimpsest traces above ⌒.

4.a   Traces:

5.a   So G 1923:23, BF:85. Contra VG pl.9a (?); S:12* ( ). ⟩ apparently corrected, from a high ⌒ or ⌓.

9.a   B1 156–7 is obscure: V:115 read , VG pl.9a ,   Palimpsest G 1923:23 ?? , noting that 'w has been corrupted into a form resembling ⌇'; S:14* . Dévaud read as *jḫt–nbt* (Grapow 1913:746), but unlikely. Perhaps read ?

10.a   Traces:

11.a   So VG pl.9a, BF:66. Contra S:14* ( ).

B1

R

B1

R

B1 5

R

B1

R

B1

R 10

B1

R

1.a   So G 1923:23. Contra VG pl.9a, S:14* (⌇𝔦⌇).

3.a–b   Placed thus: S:14–5* reads with B1 159 (*m h3w ntj jm=k*), groundlessly.

3.c   ⌒ was written near top of line, then rewritten, more cursively, lower down. Contra BF:67 *et al.* (⌒).

7.a   So G 1923:23, traces of an erasure or palimpsest above.

10.a Traces of an erased sign (or palimpsest ?) after ⦀ .

10.b   So VG pl.4a, BF:67; not ⦀ or 𝔦 .

167

| | B1 |
| 26.3 26.2 | R |

168

| | B1 |
| 26.5 26.4 | R |

169

| | B1 | 5 |
| 26.7 26.6 | R | |

170

| | B1 |
| 27.1 26.8 | R |

171

| | B1 |
| 27.2 | R | 10 |

173 172

| | B1 |
| 27.3 | R |

1.a   Contra VG pl.9a (○).

1.b   Contra S:14* (▦); palimpsest traces above   .

2.a The line endings of column 26 are all fragmentary; any further lost signs here unlikely.

3.a   Nothing lost (G 1923:23)

3.b   Contra S:14* (▭◦).

4.a Probably nothing lost; one group at most.

8.a   Traces:

10.a Traces:

11.a   So G 1923:23, BF:68. Contra VG pl.9a (○).

174

B1

27.5   27.4

R

176   175

B1

27.6

R

177

B1   5

27.8   27.7

R

178

B1

R

179

B1

181   180   10

182

184   183

185

1.a   So V:124, Gilula 1978:129. Contra G 1923:23, S:14*, BF:68 ( ).

1.b   So BF:68; cf. 33a.13.a, 38a.7.b, 38a.8.b, 40a.5.a, 40a.6.a, M.466. 'Certainly not the ordinary ; it looks more like ←' (G 1923:23).

2.a   Traces:

7.a   So G 1923:23. Contra VG pl.10a ( ).

8.a   Traces:

8.b   So BF:68. Contra VG pl.4a ( ).

9.a   A short , written over a : a correction or, more probably, palimpsest.

9.b   Contra V:128, VG pl.10a, S:14* ( ); resemblance to is due to surface. Cf. 23a.5.a.

10.a   So BF:68. Contra VG pl.10a et al.( ).

10.b   No trace of tick; emend to .

11.a   So G 1923:23. Contra Gunn (BF:).

13.a   Traces: So BF:69. Contra S:16–7* ( ).

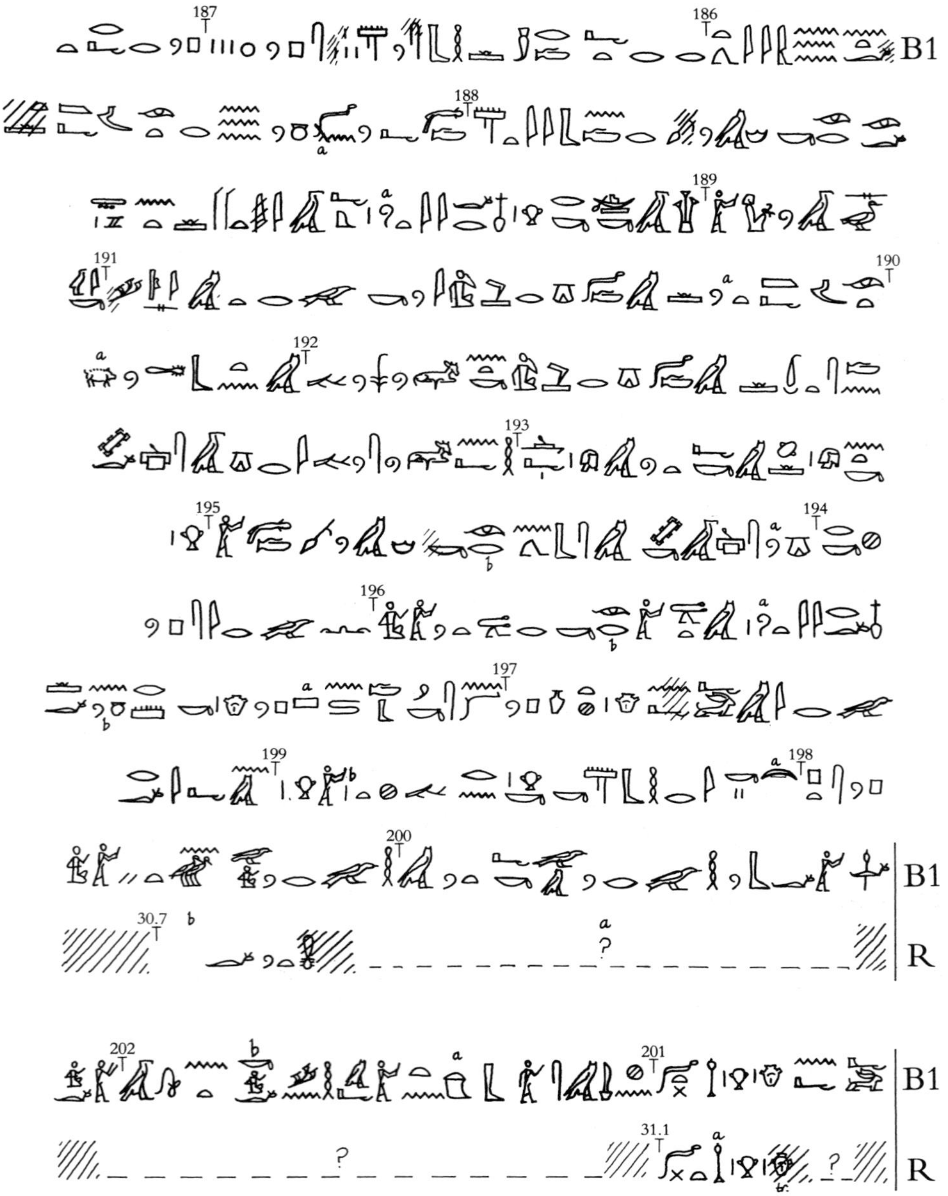

2.a   Apparently a stroke thus.

3.a   〔glyph〕   So BF:69; alternative suggestion of VG pl.10a (〔glyph〕) is unlikely.

4.a   〔glyph〕   So G 1923:23, BF:69. Contra V:133 (〔glyph〕); VG pl.10a (〔glyph〕).

5.a   See 23a.5.c.

7.a   Or perhaps an erroneous 〔glyph〕 ?

7.b   Small, like 〔glyph〕 .

8.a   See 3.a.

8.b   See 7.b.

9.a   〔glyph〕

9.b   〔glyph〕   'Ob nicht eher 〔glyph〕 ?' (VG pl.11a, comparing 〔glyph〕 in B1 233). Resemblance to // may be due to being written over a palimpsest trace.

10.a   〔glyph〕   Or 〔glyph〕 ?

10.b   The | is distinct from 〔glyph〕 in line above (contra B I,100).

12.a   Traces: 〔glyph〕   The end of R 30.4 may read 〔glyph〕 (=B1 199), and R 30.5 〔glyph〕 (=B1 199).

12.b   Probably nothing lost.

13.a   〔glyph〕   So BF:69; cf. Faulkner 1956:25 n.113a–b. Contra V:139 (〔glyph〕)S:16* (〔glyph〕 ; cf. Blackman 1934:219).

13.b   〔glyph〕   Contra S:16* (〔glyph〕 ; cf. Blackman 1934:219).

14.a   So BF:69; cf. M.447 (Bulaq 18). Contra VG pl.4 bis a *et al.* (〔glyph〕).

203 | B1
× 7 31.2 a? | R

204 a | B1
? br. × 4 31.3 ? | R

205 | B1
31.5 ? br. 4½? a? 31.4 | R

207 | B1
1¼? 31.6 ?c b 2½? a | R
br.

208 | B1
br. 31.7 ? | R

209 | B1
31.8 ? | R

1.a   ✕ added later, overlapping ⬚ .

2.a   Size of these lacunae uncertain; R 30.7–8 suggest that they are larger than as shown in VG pl.4 bis.

3.a   ⬚   So BF:70. Contra VG pl.11a *et al.* (⬚).

6.a   Traces: ⬚   Contra VG pl.4a bis (⬚ ?).
                        Following traces: ⬚

8.a   Traces: ⬚

8.b   Traces: ⬚

8.c   ⬚   So BF:70, VG pl.4 bis a. Or ❘❘❘ ?

B1

210

212
211

213 a

214

215
5

216

217

a 218

b
a
219

220 a
10

222
221

?b
a
223

224

225

227
226
15

3.a So VG pl.11a, S:16*, B II,3. Contra G 1923:23 ('hardly be ⮷ or ⮵ ', mislead by blot above).

8.a B1 218–87 are vertical lines.

9.a Contra Sethe 1928a:23 1.20 n.1 (⮶ ; cf. Sethe 1927:30).

9.b Large, like ⬯.

10.a See 9.b.

12.a

12.b

B1

5

10

15

3.a Traces: So VG pl.12a, BF:71. No indication that it is palimpsest (contra G 1923:23).

3.b Written   , with traces of a ⌒ under , later erased.

4.a Traces: So BF:71, G 1923:23.
Contra V:155, VG pl.12a ( );
S:18–9* ( ).

5.a So VG pl.12a, very cursive.

6.a   So VG pl.12a, BF:71. Contra S:18* ( ).

8.a Reading certain.

10.a   So BF:72. Contra VG pl.12a. A tick is part of in B1 259, 270 (although not in B1 142); here right tick is merged with broad lower stroke.

10.b Large like ⌒.

12.a Contra S:20–1* ( ).

13.a   So V:160, BF:72. Contra S:20* ( ).

15.a   Contra S:20* ( ).

B1

5

10

B1

B2

15

1.a   So VG pl.12a *et al.* Contra S:20* (⸗ ; cf. 25a.11a).

2.a   So VG pl.12a *et al.* Contra S:20* (⸗ ; cf. B1 265).

3.a   The ligature ⸗ is treated as if ⸗ .

5.a   Placed after ⸗ due to lack of space.

10.a   Previous traces are certain. Following traces much clearer in *LD* VI,109.

11.a   Illegible traces: Perhaps restore ⸗ ?

11.b   Contra VG pl.13a, S:20*, BF:72 (⸗).

12.a   Contra S:20* (⸗).

13.a   So M.466, BF:72; see 28a.1.b, 38a.7.b, 38a.8.b, 40a.5.a, 40a.6.a.

15.a   Traces?   Perhaps of another group before line end (⸗)?

B1

B2

B1

B1

B1

B1

B2

B1

B2

5

10

2.a   Certainly the end of a line (see fig. 5).

11.a   So G 1923:24, S:22*, BF:73; not ⌣ (suggested by VG pl.13a).

12.a   See fig.5. 𝔸s cramped, and 𝄐 written to left, to avoid line
       end. Number of groups lost based on comparison with B2 1.

13.a   [hieroglyph] (fibres misaligned as mounted).

14.a   Traces level with [hieroglyphs] : [hieroglyphs]

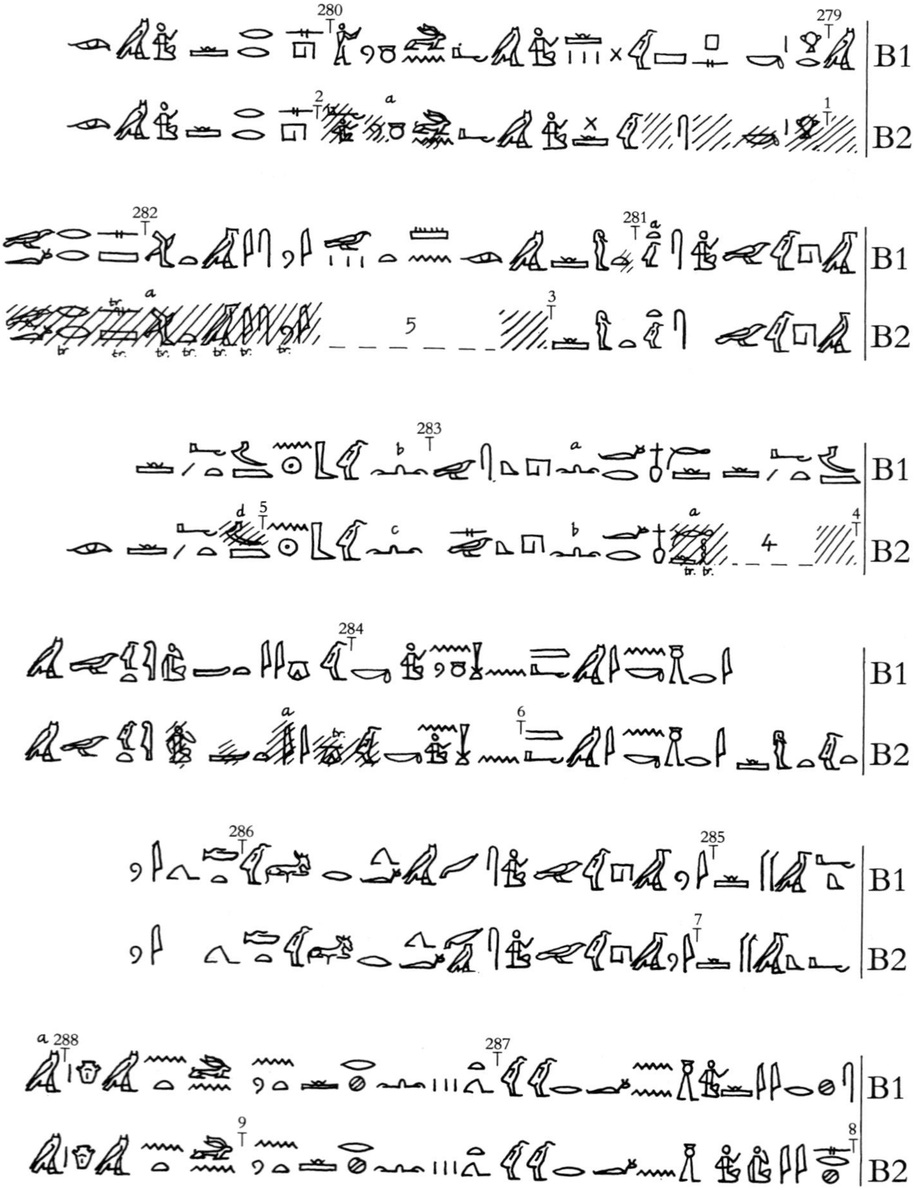

2.a   Traces:

3.a   Traces of a ⌒ to the left between ⌒ and 𝄇 , either palimpsest or a correction.

4.a   Traces:

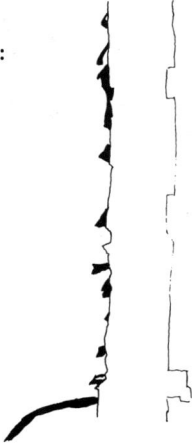

5.a   So VG pl.14a *et al.*
Contra S:22* (⋂⋂⋃⋃).

5.b   So VG pl.14a *et al.*
Contra S:22* (⟶).

6.a   Traces:

6.b   So VG pl.18a; see 5.a.   6.c   So VG pl.18a; see 5.b.

6.d   Possibly room for another sign (so BF:74), but doubtful.

8.a   Traces:

11.a   Beginning of verso. Bl 288–335 written in columns of horizontal lines.

[Hieroglyphic text in parallel registers B1 and B2, with line numbers 289, 290, 291, 292, 293, 294 (B1) and 10, 11, 12, 13, 14, 15, 16, 17 (B2); marginal line numbers 5 and 10]

1.a   So G 1923:24 ('the det.s of *jwsw* in [B1 333, 354] are somewhat similar'). Contra VG pl.14a (suggesting ⟨…⟩); S:22* (⟨…⟩).

2.a   Traces: So G 1923:24 ('no trace of ⌢ but a small horizontal sign (ııı?) after ⟨…⟩'), BF:74. Contra VG pl.18a (⟨…⟩). Palimpsest traces also present.

2.b   See 1.a.

3.a   So G 1923:24, BF:174. Contra S:22* (⟨…⟩); S:157 (⟨…⟩).

4.a   Traces: (collated with *LD* VI,113), apparently wiped away. Contra VG pl.18a, BF:74 (⟨…⟩; cf. G 1923:24).

7.a   A stroke joining ⟨…⟩ and ⟨…⟩ .

9.a   So VG pl.14a, BF:75 *et al.* 'C[oul]d be ⟨…⟩' (B II,22). Contra Faulkner 1962:296 (⟨…⟩).

9.b   Or ⟨…⟩?

10.a   So VG pl.18a, BF:75 *et al.*; see 9.a.

B1
B2

B1
B2

B1
B2   5

B1
B2

B1
B2   10

B1
B2

1.a Long like .

5.a  So G 1923:24; cf. in B1 220. Contra VG pl.14a ( ). Short line ending column.

6.a Traces:  Contra VG pl.18a ( ); unread in G 1923:4 *et al.* Cf. B2 25.

9.a Widely spaced, with near the top of the line, perhaps to avoid damaged surface.

10.a Traces:  (collated with *LD* VI,113).

12.a Blot to right of group.

12.b Written  to avoid long line.

	B1
	B2
	B1
	B2
	B1
	B2
	B1
	B2
	B1
	B2
	B1
	B2

1.a **ᑌ** Clearly thus; no palimpsest.

3.a **⟶** ▭ corrected over ᐃ∼ ?

7.a After this line two lines were written (=B1 310–2), then erased, leaving a short column (see fig.4).

7.b **⟶** So VG pl.15a, BF:76; cf. 28a.1.b, 33a.13.a, 38a.8.b, 40a.5.a, 40a.6.a.

8.a **ᒪ** So BF:76. Contra VG pl.19a (🐦).

8.b **⟶** So BF:76; see 7.b.

11.a Traces: **ᒪ**

5

10

3.a Traces: [hieroglyph]   So VG pl.15a, BF:76. Contra S:24* ([hieroglyph]).

3.b [hieroglyph]   See 36a.1.a. So BF:76. Contra S:24* ([hieroglyph]).

4.a [hieroglyph]   See 36a.2.b. So BF:76. Contra S:25* ([hieroglyph]).

4.b Written to one side to avoid long line/edge.

7.a [hieroglyphs]   So VG pl.15a *et al.* Contra
                     S:24* ([hieroglyphs]).

8.a Written [hieroglyphs] . So G 1923:24 (contra VG pl.15a, adding | | |).

8.b So VG pl.19a; see 7.a.

12.a [hieroglyph]   So G 1923:24, BF:77. Contra S:25* ([hieroglyph]).

³¹⁵ ...	B1
⁴⁴ ... ⁴³ ...	B2

^{a 316} ...	B1
⁴⁵ ...	B2

^b ^a ³¹⁷ ...	B1
^a ⁴⁶ ...	B2

5

³¹⁸ ...	B1
^{a 48} ... ⁴⁷ ...	B2

³²⁰ ... ³¹⁹ ...	B1
⁴⁹ ...	B2

10

³²¹ ...	B1
⁵¹ ... ^a ... ⁵⁰ ...	B2

3.a   So VG pl.15a *et al.* Contra S:24* (〰), who reads thus in following lines in B1 and B2. The signs are:

B1:   B2:

5.a   So BF:77; see 28a.1.b, 33a.13.a, 38a.7.b, 38a.8.b, 40a.6.a.

5.b   Or 〰?

5.c   Unread in BF:77 *et al.* So Gunn (BF) 'from some confusion w[ith] *pḏ* "sharpen"?'. Contra S:24–5* (〰 'un oeil blanc').

6.a   So BF:77; see 5.a.

6.b   So G 1923:24 *et al.* Or 〰?

8.a Blot thus:

12.a   〰 corrected out of |||.

322

|B1

52

|B2

323

|B1

53 a

|B2

324 a

b |B1   5

b   55   a   54

|B2

325

|B1

56

|B2

326 a

|B1

58   c   b   a   57

|B2   10

327 a

|B1

59
a

|B2

4.a   Written [glyphs] to avoid long line/edge.

5.a   Contra VG pl.16a ([glyphs]); the stroke is a *:k* that was first written to the left of *ꜥw³*, then erased and rewritten underneath.

5.b   [glyph]   (collated with *LD* VI,110). So BF:78 *et al*. Contra VG pl.16a ([glyph]).

6.a   Section heavily damaged, to be restored after *LD* VI,113:

6.b   Blot (see 6.a).

9.a   [glyph]   So Gunn (MS). Contra VG pl.16a *et al*. ([glyph]).

10.a Traces, clear in *LD* VI,113: Contra VG pl.20a ([glyph]).

10.b [glyph]   So Gunn (MS). Contra VG pl.20a *et al*. ([glyph]).

10.c Trace, clear in *LD* VI,110.

11.a Short line ending column.

11.b [glyphs]   So VG pl.16a, BF:78 *et al*. Contra Luft 1983:141 ([glyph]).

12.a [glyph]   So VG pl.20a, BF:78 *et al*.; see 11.b.

B1

B2

B1

B2

B1   5

B2

B1

B2

B1

B2   10

B1

B2

3.a   So VG pl.16a, BF:79 *et al*. Contra Luft 1983:141 (⬮). Perhaps corrected out of ⌓ .

3.b   So VG pl.16a, BF:79. Contra S:26* (⬮). Cf. B1 330, B2 123.

4.a   So VG pl.20a, BF:79 *et al.*; see 3.a.

4.b   So VG pl.20a, BF:79. Contra S:27* (⬮). Cf. B2 63.

4.c   So G 1923:24 ('a low wide form found elsewhere eg. [B2] 85 top'), BF:79. Contra S:27* ('*n* dittog.').

8.a   Written ⬮ to avoid long line/edge.

9.a   Contra G 1923:24, BF:79 (⬮); S:26* (⬮). ⬮ corrected over ⬮ ; hence cramped form of second ⬮ . No trace of any ⬮ ; palimpsest traces also present.

9.b

10.a   So BF:79. Contra VG pl.20a (suggesting ⬮ and ⬮ ; cf. 37a.5.a).

11.a   So S:26* (although the orthography with ⬮ is unusual: Grapow 1913:743). Contra VG pl.16a (⬮ + blot); BF:79 (⬮). ⬮ has a tick like ⬮ .

12.a   So VG pl.20a. Contra S:27* (⬮); BF:79 (⬮).

B1
B2

B1
B2

B1   5
B2

B1
B2

B1
B2   10

B1
B2

1.a   ⸢ᵱ⸣ and ⸢◦⸣ widely spaced due to blot between. Palimpsest traces also at bottom of column and in B1 334.

4.a   Traces: ⸢𓀒⸣ .

4.b   ⸢𓏤⸣ clear (contra G 1923:24: ⸢𓅨⸣ 'unusual in form').

5.a   Short line ending short column. B1 336–57 are vertical lines.

6.a   Contra B II,39 ('prob. only one group [after / ◦] ie ⸢𓄿⸣'.

7.a   ⸢𓋴𓏏⸣   So BF:80. Contra VG pl.17a (suggesting ⸢𓂝₁?⸣). ǀ is corrected out of ◦ .

7.b   ⸢𓃀⸣   ⸢𓃀⸣ corrected out of ⌒ .

8.a   ⸢𓃀⸣   So G 1923:24, BF:80. Contra VG pl.21a (ǀ).

9.a   Written to left to avoid long line.

B1

B2

B1

B2

B1 5

B2

B1

B2

B1

B2 10

B1

B2

1.a   [hieroglyph]   Contra Gunn (BF: [hieroglyph]).

3.a   Added to right of line by scribe who started to write ⸢[hieroglyphs]⸣ as in B2.

5.a   [hieroglyph]   Contra VG pl.17a *et al.* ([hieroglyph]).

5.b   [hieroglyph]   So BF:80.

6.a   [hieroglyph]   So BF:80; cf. 46a.3.a.

6.b [hieroglyph] clear in *LD* VI,114. Room to restore [hieroglyph] , if a slightly long line.

9.a [hieroglyph] written over an erased [hieroglyphs].

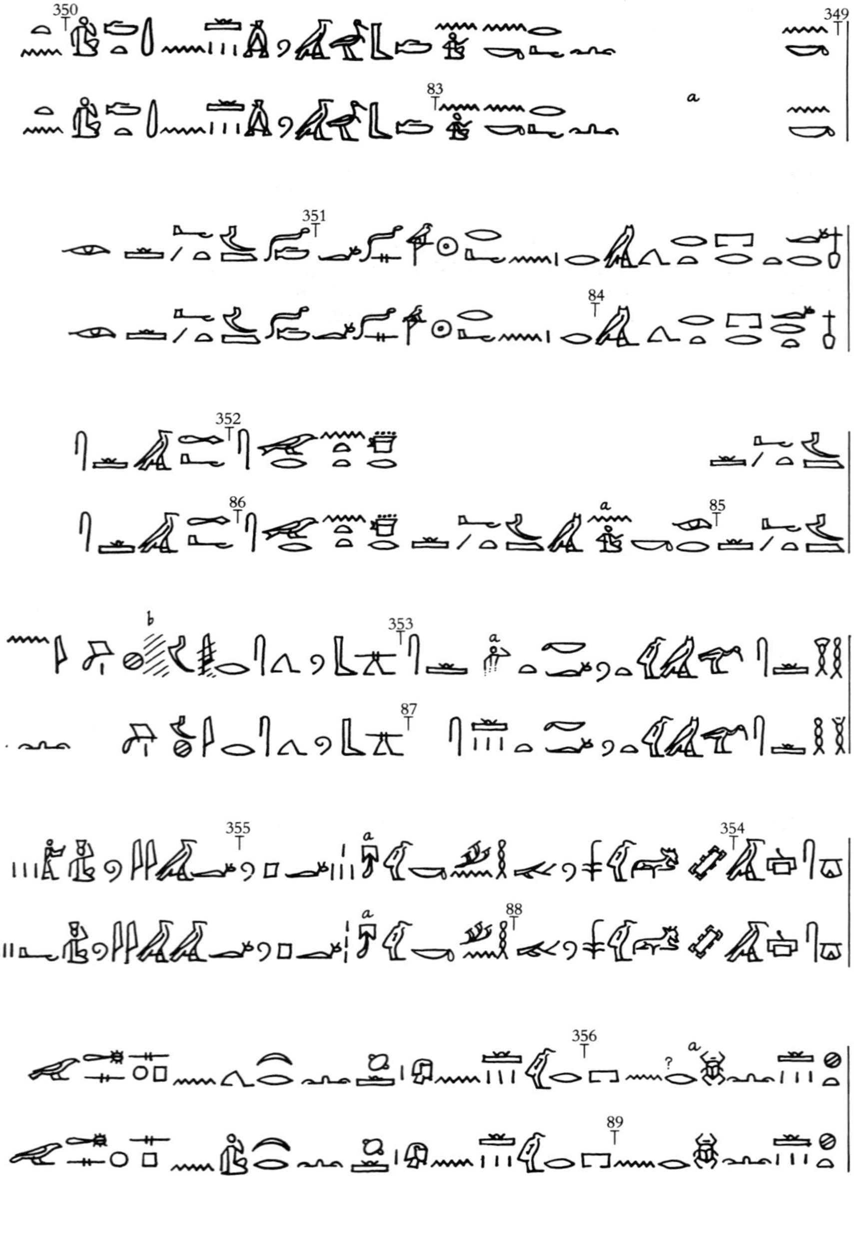

B1 / B2

2.a   Blank space 3–4 groups long. Traces (cf. *LD* VI,114):
Either signs purposely obliterated, or palimpsest
traces, over which scribe would not write.
Almost certainly the former; probably another negative
phrase was written here and then erased.

6.a   So G 1923:24, BF:81. Contra VG pl.21a ( ).

7.a   Contra S:26* ( ); left blank in VG pl.17a *et al.*
Not a misformed , but a correction; perhaps the
scribe started to write , then realized his
mistake, and wrote over the half finished sign.
 written to left to avoid long line.

7.b   Probably no loss between and . There is an
erroneous stroke, like a , through .

9.a   So James 1962:139–40. Contra VG pl.17a (?); G
1923:24, BF:81 (, comparing *Tb.* (Naville) 125
Schlussrede 32 Ca); S:28–9* (?, 'peut–être un vase').

10.a   Contra VG pl.21a *et al.*; see 9.a.

11.a   So VG pl.17a, BF:81; cf. B1 313. Or with no ?

B1

B2

B2

5

10

1.a   So VG pl.17a *et al.* Contra S:28* ( ).

2.a   So VG pl.21a *et al.*; see 1.a.   3.a   So BF:81; cf. 44a.6.a.

5.a   So VG pl.22a, BF:82. Contra S:28* ( ).

5.b Traces: *LD* VI,114:

note distortion of fibres. Unread in VG pl.22a *et al.* 'The suggestion *bjn tnm* [VG pl.22a] is impossible' (G 1923:24). The first vertical sign is damaged. The last sign looks like ; for the twist on the sign above cf. 47a.10.a.

J. Osing reads *s3w shm-grg* ('Principiis Obsta (Bauer B2, 95–97)', in *Egypt: Temple of the Whole World / Ägypten: Tempel der gesamten Welt: Studies in Honour of Jan Assmann*, Sibylle Meyer (ed.), 283–6. Leiden and Boston: Brill 2003).

6.a   So VG pl.22a *et al.* Contra S:28 ( ).

7.a   So VG pl.22a *et al.* Contra S:28–9*( ).   7.b   So G 1923:24, BF:82.

7.c   So VG pl.22a *et al.* Contra S:28* (; cf. 40a.3.a).   7.d   Contra G 1923:24, BF:82 ( ); S:28* ( ). Perhaps a misformed (cf. P Prisse 7.11)?

9.a   Faint traces (collated with *LD* VI,114). So G 1923:24 ('highly probable'), BF:82. Restore (S:28*), or (just enough space).

9.b   Collated with *LD* VI,114 . So BF:82; 'for an approximation of the det. of *hwd* to , see *Adm*.8.2. The correction in the margin is clearly ' (G 1923:24). Faulkner transcribed the misformed determinative as (1962:186). Contra S:28–9* ('la correction marginale est double: 1. le trait complétant 2. le signe complétant *w(t)*(?)'; cf. Blackman 1934:219).

fainter ink

10.a   III corrected over (?).

12.a   Palimpsest traces above .

14.a   written over another sign – perhaps a badly formed which was rewritten more distinctly.

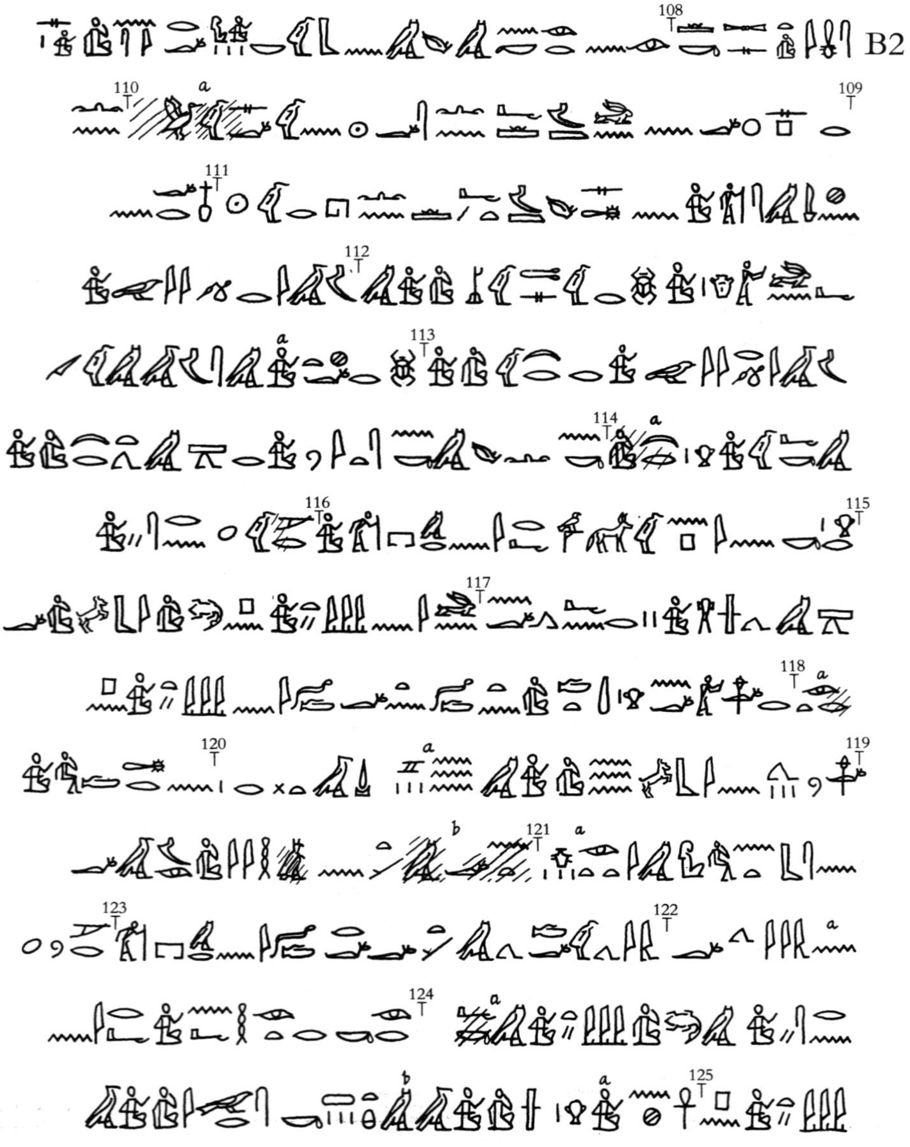

2.a   Traces: Restore (BF:82). Written thus to avoid long line/edge.

5.a   So BF:82. Contra G 1923:24 ([M.49]; cf. M.33 [Sinuhe]).

6.a   Traces:

9.a   Traces:

10.a   So G 1923:24 ('the middle 〰 has a peculiar twist at right end, the effect of which is exagerated by loss of fibres'), BF:83. Contra V:228 ( ); S:30 ( ). Middle 〰 is distinct from (contra VG pl.23a); cf. B2 120.

11.a   Traces at line end: So BF:83. Contra VG pl.13a ( ).

11.b   Faint traces (collated with *LD* VI,114): So G 1923:24, BF:83. Contra VG pl.23a (suggesting).

12.a   So VG pl.23a; not 〰. No trace of after (contra VG pl.23a).

13.a   No further loss; traces:

14.a   Full form; an error for ?

14.b   Written to one side; perhaps added later?

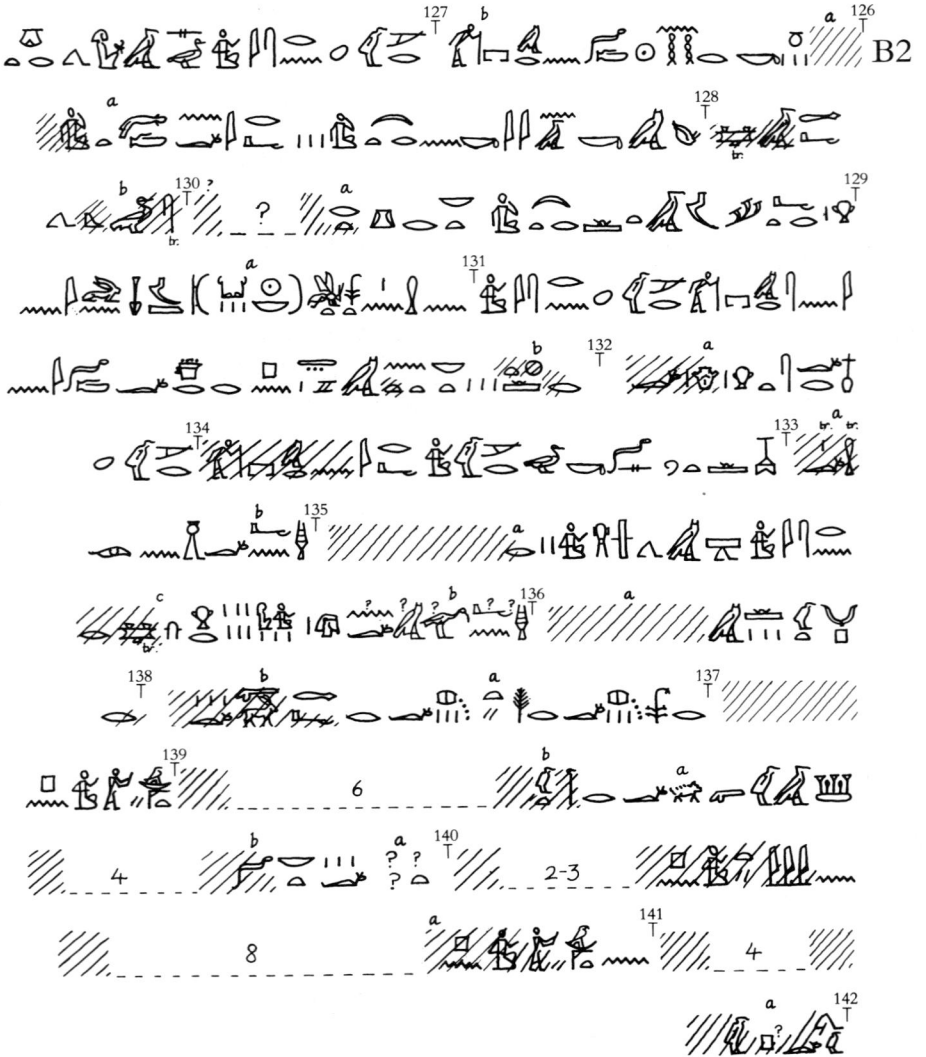

1.a Traces, collated with *LD* VI,113:
So G 1923:24–5 ('▨▨▨ seems probable'). Restore
⌒ᵢᵢᵢ▢▢◊; there is little room for any ◊ (contra S:30*).
The group has completely vanished, but is not
'purposely expunged' (contra B II,52); cf. lacunae
B2 130, 132

1.b Short line (by c.2.5 groups). Read *ḏḏ.<j>n*; apparently no loss
(cf. *LD* VI,113).

2.a Traces: (collated with *LD* VI,113). So G 1923:25;
contra VG pl.23a (suggesting ⌒▢◊⌒).
For form of 🐍 cf. B2 79. Uncertain if any
lacuna thereafter, but probable (BF:83).

3.a Traces: So G 1923:25. Contra VG pl.23a (▨▨◊▢).
Room to restore ◊▨ or ◊ (as Sethe
1928a:28 1.10); possibly no further loss.

3.b Traces: So G 1923:25. Contra V:230, VG pl.23a
(⌒▢◊▢).

4.a Written so that B2 131–2 are widely spaced:

5.a Traces: Restore ⌒×◊ , with short line (G 1923:25,
BF:83). Contra V:230 ([⌒× ⸗ ◊).

5.b Traces certain.

6.a Traces:

7.a Traces: Restore 🐍◊⸗◊ ⌒ ◊, with long line like B1
132, unless written to one side (G 1923:25,
BF:83). Contra V:231 (⌒× ⌒ ◊).

7.b Traces: (collated with *LD* VI,113). So G 1923:25, BF:83.

8.a This lacuna too small to restore ⌒ᵢᵢᵢ◊▢◊▨ (contra V:231);
restore an item of goods. Traces:

8.b   Very faint. Unread in VG pl.24a, G 1923:25, BF:83, save for last two signs (⎵⎵ᵇ); of which S:30* read ⁣⁣⁣ as ↶. The suggestion *ḫrw=f* (V:231) is impossible. ⁣⁣⁣ written to left.

8.c   Traces:

9.a   So BF:83. Contra VG pl.24a *et al.*

9.b   Certain traces. *'3[w=f]* is probably ehough to fill lacuna, if a short line; contra Sethe 1928a:25 l.17: ⁣⁣⁣⁣⁣⁣⁣⁣⁣⁣.

10.a   After *LD* VI,113 (collated); now very faint. So G 1923:25, BF:83. Contra VG pl.24a (⁣⁣⁣⊘).

10.b   Traces:

11.a   Faint traces (collated with *LD* VI,113): VG pl.24a suggests ⁣⁣⁣⊘ , which is impossible unless arranged ⁣⁣⁣ ⁣⁣⁣⊘ . ⁣⁣⁣⊘ is possible, but unlikely in context.

11.b   Trace certain: restore either ⁣⁣⁣ or ⁣⁣⁣ .

12.a   As B2 142 begins with the start of the colophon, this probably a full line; number of groups lost uncertain, and probably widely spaced.

13.a   So G 1923:25 ('almost certain in large sprawling forms'), BF:83. Contra VG pl.24a, S:30* (⁣⁣⁣). One might expect B2 to rubricize a colophon, but rubrics are often omitted near ends of mss (Posener 1951b:76 n.5). Restore ⁣⁣⁣. Compare vertical colophons in other MK literary mss:

B2 restored	P Berlin 3022 (*Sinuhe* B) l.309	P Ermitage 1116a (*Shipwrecked Sailor*) ll.186–7	P Berlin 3024 (*Lebensmüder*) ll.154–5